The St Merino Solution

The St Merino solution
A manager's guide to profitable computing

NORMAN SANDERS

Illustrations by
TONY HART

ASSOCIATED BUSINESS PROGRAMMES
LONDON

Published by
Associated Business Programmes Ltd,
17 Buckingham Gate, London S.W.1.

First published 1978

© 1978 Norman Sanders

ISBN 0 85227 079 8

Typeset by
Molineaux [K Studios] Ltd, Coulsdon, Surrey.
Printed and bound in Great Britain by
Redwood Burn Limited, Trowbridge & Esher

To St Merino, the Patron Saint of those having the wool pulled over their eyes.

It's an old split. Like the one between art and history. One does it and the other talks about how it's done and the talk about how it's done never seems to match how one does it.

Robert Pirsig

Zen and the Art of Motor Cycle Maintenance

Contents

Apologia and acknowledgements

These chapters have emerged over a period of fifteen years and more as the result of a hobby. My job has been to make computers work, but as a necessary sideline I found it more and more necessary to get the understanding and support of my clients; in particular at the levels where the purse-strings were held. During the 1950s this wasn't a problem because what we did didn't appear to be important and it didn't cost much. But by the 1960s the computer was being taken very seriously and the bill was attracting top level attention.

This hobby started at Boeing when I found myself sitting at the Monday morning staff meeting alongside the heads of engineering, production, quality control and finance, making the amazing discovery that they knew less about the computer than the people buried a dozen levels lower in their organisations. Computing by then was deeply entrenched in their operations, and if the computer was down they stopped work. They were vulnerable, but they weren't in any way in control. So whenever anything went wrong a forest of fingers was pointed at me.

My first stumbling steps were to try to explain it all to my colleagues at Boeing, and I am eternally grateful for the opportunity. Boeing has been no ordinary user of the computer. It has been one of the pioneers amongst the pioneers, so there was a lot to explain. These first attempts were miserable failures, but with time I slowly began to understand the essential problems and to develop techniques for tackling them.

The next phase consisted of a close collaboration with Bob

Worsing in giving lectures and speeches to the American Management Association, IBM, CDC and others. This forced our attention on familiar problems in a new way. Indeed it forced us to take the necessary time to *describe* computing instead of just doing it. A very healthy discipline. We learned a lot by simply writing it down. I would like to convey my profoundest gratitude to Bob Worsing for this and a great deal else.

Then followed a two-year stint where the hobby became a full-time job, that of getting Sperry Univac's International Executive Centre going in Rome. Suddenly the audience had changed. How could we solve problems of nationality and language, type of company, size of company, different legal systems, and so on? In other words, what was the essence of computing that was common to everyone? I don't know how well we explained computing, but we certainly learned a lot about people in the attempt, and my appreciation for the opportunity of meeting such a wide variety of managers and discussing their problems into the small hours cannot be adequately expressed. However I couldn't have got the Centre going without the staunch support of people like Nick Smith, Bob Lewis, Bob Tricker, Don White, Hugh Price and Bill McCreight. There were many others who played a vital role, and it is impossible to mention them all by name, but they contributed ideas which appear, unacknowledged, in these pages.

I am deeply indebted to one man in particular, a director of finance from a company in New York who obstinately refused to understand anything. But after days of frustration I suddenly found myself on the road to Damascus. In a blinding flash of awareness I realised what his and everyone else's problem was; the computer was invisible, and almost all its works. Solve the invisibility problem and you've made it.

In realising the problem I could immediately see a solution to it, and built a visible computer which I still use in lectures. Although the visible computer itself doesn't figure in the book, the ideas that it has spawned are there.

After leaving Rome I continued with the hobby at the Nor-Data Software company, constantly revising the ideas and approach, and am grateful for the opportunities of trying them out under the auspices of the United Nations Development Program and Univac in Eastern Europe. I am also grateful to Denis Davie for invitations to Australia, which helped confirm the fact that computing is the same wherever you go, and to Tore Bough-Jensen and Jan-Petter Schoyen with whom I have had many enjoyable sessions in Scandinavia.

If your main job is doing and managing, writing can at best be a hobby, and there's little energy and time left at the end of the day in which to indulge it. To accomplish anything at all one must write fast and write once, so one needs a source of inspiration and an honest critic. I have been extremely fortunate over the years to have had both in the guise of Tony Jay, and this is just one more opportunity of thanking him for all his patience and encouragement. And, in turn, his friend Tony Hart, one who has really solved the problem of making visible the problems and frustrations of management; and in such a delightful way.

These chapters represent the latest version of a continuing evolution, and I am particularly indebted to Solveig for helping me put it in book form with such care and organisation.

Nuts and bolts

The first part of this book tells you why top management should get involved in the computing effort; something about computers themselves, though not much; what kinds of pay-off to look for, and what it all might cost. It is a dangerous thing, of course, to commit oneself on the subject of costs, especially in the field of computing. Costs vary greatly around the world, both in terms of hardware and people; they vary with time and they are very much a function of individual capability. But to omit a full discussion of costs is to shirk one's duty, because these are the first questions that any competent manager asks. The answers aren't true to the penny, but the orders of magnitude are right. More importantly, this section tries to give you a mechanism for estimating and controlling costs.

1 A prayer to St Merino

It's been a rough week. It started with a fire in the number 2 warehouse, and you spent the whole of Monday watching the firemen at work and fighting the insurance company. You couldn't sign Monday's outgoing mail until Wednesday because you had to attend the launching of your new floating oil rig on Tuesday. But Wednesday was shot out of the water because of the simultaneous visits of two hot prospects that simply couldn't be delegated to Marketing. Thursday was entirely given over to harangues with your Director of Finance and pleas with your banker, while Friday would have been a relatively peaceful day of humdrum therapy had it not been for that half-hour computing presentation at the end of the day. You had postponed your chief computer man, George Crudworthy, and his kindergarten three times already, and it wouldn't have conformed to acceptable managerial theory not to have let him in.

It was a complete waste of time of course. You didn't understand a word they said. George himself wasn't too bad. He's a bit of a nagger, of course. Always on about getting you involved, leading the effort, making the major decisions. But how can you? Look at the people he's got. The language they use. You doubt whether they wash. And they spend the company's money like a drunken sailor. Destroying the ancient traditions of this venerable institution.

You gave them a full half-hour. You were genuinely determined to concentrate your mind on their blabberings, but they didn't give you a chance. They were in asking for another hundred thousand for the CRUDCOMP project, and a six-month delay in the delivery date. But you couldn't even remember what the project was all about. Anyway, how could you possibly deny them a stay of execution if they had no means at their disposal of meeting it? You could fire George, of course, but that would only make matters worse. Either someone would have to come in cold from some other department, or one of those hairy creatures would get promoted and you'd be forced to shake him by the hand. Moreover, the company's organisation has gone through hell these last two years. Three Directors of Finance in succession with nervous breakdowns. Engineering and Manufacturing no longer speaking to one another, and the salesmen taking the stuff out the warehouse themselves because the orders weren't getting through.

They want another hundred thousand on top of the three hundred they've already spent, but you haven't seen a single shred of evidence that they've done anything with the money – except the bills. George took you on a tour of the computer room and you caught a chill from the air-conditioning which postponed your trip to Grand Cayman, but you didn't see anything worth looking at. All you could hear was the staccato clacking of the printers. While the operator was hidden behind the tape racks reading the unprintable, the printers were hard at it printing the unreadable. No solace there.

So it wasn't many minutes before your mind left the presentation and wandered over to the production line where for fifteen shifts a week Amalgamated Matchbox churned out good old substantial products for the commercial market. That's the place to go when they bother you with their problems! You wander round with your swagger cane, and old J.B.'s very presence whips up production five per cent. You can see it all happening. People tripping over one another in a frenzy of activity. The overhead crane at full speed back and forth the entire run of the building. Cardboard boxes full of the stuff piling up on the dock. Does the heart good. Solid company with a solid reputation. Plenty of evidence.

Occasionally your reverie was rudely interrupted by the plaintive voice of a pimply youth waving a slide rule at you

People tripping over one-another in a frenzy of activity.

and talking about marginal utility and linear programming.
Degree in OR, whatever that is. We're supposed to get a
return on our investment of 200 per cent by 1980 if CRUD-
COMP ever sees the light of day. But in the meantime they
need another 16 K of core, whatever that means. And George
met this Australian in a bar last night who happened to have
a brand new search algorithm in his pocket which would cut
the run time in half. But we don't even know what the old
run time is because nothing's started to run yet. You wish it
would even crawl.

You suppose that underneath it all they're doing the right
thing. You'd like to ask them a lot of penetrating questions,
but you don't know what to ask. If you did their faces would
wither with contempt, so you delegate the whole thing. That
is to say, you abdicate. You thank them for their presentation.
You hurry them out of the door. You lock it and you go
down on your knees and offer up a prayer to St Merino, the
patron saint of those who are having the wool pulled over
their eyes.

Get up man. This isn't like you, old J.B. Farrington-Gurney, man of action, leader of men, plunging in left and right wherever Amalgamated Matchbox is about to totter. You're not famous for delegating. Cr do you only delegate the nasty ones? You were in there handing cigarettes around to the firemen, why aren't you in there carrying the card trays for the keypunch girls? You made a damn good speech at the oil rig launching, why can't you give old George a helping hand with launching his CRUDCOMP?

If only St Merino would answer the call. But in case he doesn't I have penned these chapters as a modest substitute. There are indeed some very deep problems. Computing *is* different from anything else you'd encountered. It may not be the most expensive undertaking you've embarked on, nor is it taking up so much physical space. On the other hand it has an eerie silence about it — except for those infernal printers. There seems to be nothing to come to grips with. A warehouse fire is unfortunate, but at least it's something you understand. But you're damned if you understand what they mean by a reentrant compiler or an index sequential access method.

The purpose of this book is not to try to explain everything there is to explain about computing; your secretary wouldn't be able to lift it. Rather, it is to try to give you some appropriate insight into those aspects where I feel you should step in and make the strategic decisions. The reasons why you should do this are legion, but the most important is that of corporate profit, and profit is your concern more than anyone else's in the company. If you happen to be a non-profit concern, a hospital, a government department, or whatever, the same will hold. Your aim is to minimise cost, or create the best possible service within a given budget. These are both forms of profit in disguise.

Second only to profit comes organisation. Computers weren't invented in order to change people's organisations, but if you put them to substantial use they will certainly do so. Again, it is your organisation more than anyone else's, so you had better understand the animal that threatens to shake it up.

In addition to profit and organisation there are some other telling arguments for your getting involved. If you let the next level down handle things, what guarantee have you got that systems that span more than one department will be properly handled. What sort of people do you have for department heads? Angels? Or a bunch of conniving barons each out for your job at the drop of a banana skin? Information is something that flows horizontally around a company as well as up and down it. If you don't force the interdepartmental co-ordination, who will?

Another factor is that if you have a fair computing competence at the working level, amongst the people who deal with it every day, and you acquire some yourself, you will squeeze middle management between the two of you, guaranteeing a pretty swift acquisition of competence at all levels. This ought to give you the comfortable feeling that where possible computing applications show themselves, there will be someone around to spot the fact.

A final argument for the moment is that computing is tremendous fun. Someone said it's the last great adventure. If you leave the technical folks alone they can have an exciting technical career at your expense that has no guarantee of return to the company. Do you want technical high jinks or responsible, profitable corporate technology? If you're not stuck in there yourself, what guarantee do you have that the jinks won't be higher than the profit?

This book is intended for those in charge of companies divisions, departments, private and public, who want to make proper use of computers. It makes no difference whether you have a computer of your own, use the one down the street or on the other side of the globe, or whether you are a tiny outfit which needs an hour or two a day, or a giant concern running three shifts. One hour to one man may have the same relationship to actual needs as three shifts to another; the essential problems are the same. Computers are not only independent of size of organisation, but very largely of type of work, nationality and, most essential, law. It is no great problem establishing enough common ground between General Motors, the London Hospital, Aeroflot and the

Australian wool market to fill a book. An American computer technician could go to China and start productive work the next day, and the only change he'd notice would be the food. The differences between countries, types of business, sizes of organisation, legal systems and managerial styles are only exceeded by the similarity of computers, the people who work with them and the problems they are faced with. Computing must be the most universal of masonries.

So all consumers of the product, and today this means almost everyone, are faced with the same essential set of problems to be solved to get computing done properly.

Each chapter is fairly self-contained, and the book does not have a rigid structure. Many points are repeated and elaborated in later chapters. I have tried to minimise the technical terms, but have been forced to use some. However they are rapidly taking their place as part of our culture alongside wavelength, carburettor and kilowatt, and are no more difficult to understand.

The aim of this book is to get you, the user, actively involved in getting computing done the way you want it. But once you are involved, the details will be pertinent to your own situation and won't be found in any book. This is just to get you started.

2 *The non-emperor's clothes*

When you launched your new oil rig a thousand people came to watch. Tugs hooted, flags waved, the chairman's wife smashed a bottle of liquid propane on the rig's flanks, and it was not much of an exercise for the imagination to see the oil gushing forth into the pipeline. But when you cut the ribbon of the computer room after the hardware had arrived you were very much less certain what you were doing. So were the guests. George had written you a fine speech, but you delivered it in a very hesitant tone, and you kept looking fearfully over your shoulder in case something happened. But it didn't. No smash. No splash. All was still, and you crept out afterwards and led the guests off for cocktails and a change of conversation.

What was wrong? What was the problem? Why the bewilderment and undertainty? Why did you feel so uncomfortable? The trouble is that, underlying everything that has to do with computers, there is a fundamental difference from everything else you have ever experienced. The difference is that

COMPUTERS ARE INVISIBLE

even more than gravity. Computers consist of a great deal of clothing, but with no emperor inside. If you grasp this single fact you grasp the core of the whole problem, and you can proceed from there to victory over the wicked tailors.

When you buy a car, a crane or a combine, when you build a factory or lay down a pipeline, you can see what you are doing. Moreover, you can draw it, measure it, compare it, determine its capacity or its efficiency, and so on — all stations to profitability. So it comes as a terrible shock to be told that after all these millenia of human progress we've finally come to the point where we fork out money for something that isn't there. And that after having it for some time it's become obsolete and has to be replaced by a new one — that even more so, isn't there. You may protest that you've raised hundreds of square feet of your floor area and that it is covered with polychromatic cabinets, all douched in well-conditioned air. But open a door and what do you see? Wires mostly, and lots of very tiny electronic components. All very stationary. And if you could peel back one more skin of the onion you would be able to see something called logic. It is only at the level of logic that the computer starts to become meaningful, but logic is also the level of invisibility.

It is true that you can weigh the cabinets, measure the lengths of wire they contain, read off the amount of electric power being consumed and the temperature of the outgoing air, and so on. But the computer down the road may be lighter, contain less wire, use less power and warm up fewer sparrows, yet perform precisely the same amount of work per hour. So the clothing is irrelevant, it is the logic that's important.

You cannot measure logic. There is no computing equivalent of the inch, the pound, the volt or the horsepower. No objective measurement. No emperor. The closest you can come to depicting him is to talk about 'the things we do around here, in our own particular way'. The man down the road does things differently, and he measures his computer in a different way according to *his* lights.

But this essential invisibility affects everything it touches. A modern King Midas who's gone off the gold standard. You can't see people working; the chap who seems to be asleep may be far more productive than his neighbour feverishly creating flow charts. It is doubtful whether there will ever be a satisfactory legal mechanism; it's even less visible to the judge than it is to you, and since you can't see it you can't tell whether it's been stolen or not. A great deal of the paper that your company once used in its daily round has been replaced by magnetic tape, unreadable to the human eye.

The only way to look inside the computer at all is to get away from the machine room altogether and use a terminal of some sort. Rather like shaving with a telescope, half a mile from the mirror.

Rather like shaving with a telescope, half a mile from the mirror.

Computers have something to do with information and communication. We use them to squeeze information out of raw numbers and to send the outcome to where it's needed, quickly, accurately, appropriately and all the other good adverbs. In doing this we rid ourselves of paper files and replace them with electronic files. The computer creates all sorts of new reports about our company and how it's doing. We can even have it give us advice on how to do it better. In short we use the compiler as a communication device. But thereby hangs a paradox. The compiler certainly helps to solve the communication problems that already exist, but in doing so it creates some new ones of its own volition, often of even greater magnitude.

Again, this is because of its inherent invisibility. When you talk about traditional things you have a lot of substance to help you, a lot of non-verbal aids to communication. To explain chess to a youngster you indicate rows and columns with a flick of the wrist, and the moves by simply carrying them out.

But there's no computing equivalent of the eyes and fingers. Everything has to be explained in deep, precise detail. And this is true man to man and man to machine. There's no such thing as a vague idea. Things can't be roughly alike. It's all black and white. Either something is completely described or it isn't, and if it isn't there is always room for mis-understanding.

A particular problem child is describing the computer itself. When we buy a motor car we have a list of choices that our wives help us make. Price, station wagon or not, horse-power, colour and seat material. A list this short can be long enough to break up the happy home, but supposing you had a choice of spark plugs, distributor caps, brake linings, pedal hinges, carburettors and nuts and bolts, what an unthinkable task you'd have buying a car! Even worse, suppose there were no method of guaranteeing that you hadn't forgotten anything. The brakes for example.

But this is precisely what happens when we buy a computer. We have to specify precisely what we want from a list of hundreds of components, almost all of which are invisible. And there is never any guarantee that something vital hasn't been forgotten, or that some trivial omission hasn't reduced its performances by ninety per cent.

So the invisibility problem has forced an *increase* in the amount of information bandied about the company. There's no arm-waving any more. Everything from now on must be described in dry, precise sentences, aided by detailed drawings.

The clothing takes many forms. Some of it contains the non-emperor, some of it describes him. But as clever as we may be at the sartorial art, we will never eliminate the essential problem. Although he isn't there he makes his presence felt at every turn, and most of the particular problems described in the ensuing chapters are manifestations of the fundamental problem. The solutions proffered are the best I know of at the time of writing. As time goes on we find better ones, and sometimes they get so universally accepted that we dignify them with the appellation, science. But science is the study of the visible.

3 Taking your team with you

Let's take you momentarily back a couple of years to the placid days before you'd ever clapped eyes on George Crudworthy or any of his works. It's going to be a field day in the board room. On the left you have the board itself, the solid pillars of the business community who won their spurs when you were just a lad in the mail room, and who are still wearing them today. On the right, the department managers, badly run down and in need of a rest, who really haven't the time to be here at all, but somebody has to make sure that the board doesn't actually decide anything.

And in the middle, you, with an unusually satisfied smile on your face. You've got a bombshell in your briefcase for once, and you're going to make the most of it. You look across at the Colonel. He had his day once. Electric light. It was a struggle, though. Had to fight a terrible battle with those who regretted the passing of the smell of gas. But he's here to support you. You've flown him over from your British subsidiary for the occasion. He doesn't understand what you're up to, but he's extracted a guarantee from you that you won't bring back the gas. His monocle is misty with nostalgia.

It's time to start.

'Gentlemen,' you say. 'I have some very good news this morning and I'm happy to see so many of you able to be here.' This is followed by five minutes of rhubarb about historical occasions, shades of your founders, the spirit of progress, etc. at Amalgamated Matchbox and then the denoument.

'Gentlemen, I am profoundly moved to report to you that our company has ordered an electronic computer.'

The Colonel slowly smacks his hand on the table. The morning after Mafeking Night. His colleagues beam and nod at one another and slowly take up a visual round of applause. You thank them with a suspicion of a bow. Then you turn to the gentlemen of the line, but as you do so your smile assumes a certain wanness. Manufacturing and Engineering, normally hardly on speaking terms, appear to be asking one another for the next quadrille. Old Quality Control has lost all self-control, and a tear is seen to trickle down his care-worn cheeks. Finance's tongue is clicking like a cricket as he tries to reach for words of some sort. Only Marketing is able to utter any, and they are heavily laced with expletives acquired as a youth from the bargees on the Liffey. Translated, what he says is roughly this, 'Well J.B. you've done it this time right enough. I take it that you and the board are quite clear about what you are doing, and that you will in due course let us know what this computer is going to do for us – unless, of course, it's going to replace us altogether.'

'I say,' you say. 'That's a bit hard, Marketing. In fact that's a down-right negative attitude if ever I heard one. I mean, dammit all, it's for your own good, amongst others. I would have expected a slightly better reaction from one who's always complaining about the lack of response and support that goes on around here.'

'Look J.B.,' says Marketing, 'I don't want to spoil your finest hour, and I'm as much for innovation as the next man.' Finance's clicking reaches a crescendo. 'Even more than the next man. But there's no need to take wild leaps into the bog.'

'Quite right, Marketing,' murmurs Engineering. 'I presume that's not what we are doing. I presume that when I return to my office my people will have taken up their electronic cudgels, with the banner of design automation at the mast head.'

'Hold hard, Engineering,' you interrupt. 'It doesn't happen instantaneously you know. These things take a little time.'

'How long, J.B.?' asks Manufacturing.

'Well the salesman says he can have the equipment here in six months if we get a move on with the raised floor and the air conditioning,' you reply.

'And that's all I suppose he said we'd have to do to get ready for it,' says Manufacturing.

But there's no need to take wild leaps into the bog.

'Well, I suppose there'll be a little programming to do,' you reply, a little uneasily. Really, you hadn't bothered much about these technical details, and the salesman didn't feel that you need be bothered; a man in your position. 'But you chaps can take care of the technical details. That's what you're paid for after all. All of us of Amalgamated Matchbox have had our stint of the details you know.'

'It'll be much better for your eyes you know.' The meeting is suddenly interrupted as the Colonel leans forward and utters this unexpected sentence in a slow trembling voice.

'What will?' you asked, a trifle irritated.

'Electricity,' triumphs the Colonel, smashing the table, the blood of battle rising in his veins after half a century of quiessence. 'Thank you Colonel.' You cut him short rather acidly and turn back to the growing storm.

'Quite frankly, I think you've been just a trifle hasty J.B.,' says Quality Control.

'Couldn't you have consulted with us before you took this step?' asks Marketing.

'I seem to sense a feeling of antipathy, Gentlemen.' You wade into the attack. 'I think it's a little ungrateful. You're all busy people, and it's my job to help you as much as I can. I'm trying to take the load off a bit. After all, it's you who have the problems and do all the complaining. Whose fault is it that there's an enormous heap of left-hand threaded bolts taking up half the executive parking lot?'

'But a computer isn't going to shovel them up,' replies Manufacturing.

'But it'll stop such things happening again. We'll have an automatic ordering system based on an automated production plan, based in turn on orders obtained by Sales.' You are word-perfect in the patter, and clearly one up at this point.

'You wouldn't get a thing like that running before I've retired,' replies Manufacturing.

'We're probably the only firm in our branch that isn't already doing it.' You know you're safe here because they're too busy ever to find out what the competition is up to.

'And where are we going to put it?' asks Engineering.

'I'm glad you asked me that question. The salesman had a good look around during the weekend, and he came to the conclusion that your corner would be the best place to put it. And I feel that this is an appropriate decision since it is you, as a matter of fact, who have been pushing the hardest to get a computer.'

'It appears I've pushed a bit too hard,' replies Engineering. 'I wasn't advocating a *fait accompli.* And where do I go? And my troops?'

'We thought the disused hangar across the airfield could be converted into quite cosy engineering offices. It'll have the additional salutary effect of stopping you and Manufacturing arguing all day.' you reply.

'If that happens I'll have to double my staff overnight,' cuts in Quality Control.

'Now don't you start, Q.C. Who's always complaining about the lack of feedback? We never have an up to date picture of the work in progress. Our rework statistics are useless because they're months late.' You're word-perfect in Quality Control's speech.

'You'll never have an up to date picture of the work in progress on the computer either. At least you can put your walking boots on and take a look at what's going on out in the factory, but you'll never see a thing worth looking at in any computer room.' This remark is lost on you and most of the others at the time. But later on you begin to realise that Quality Control had done his homework on this point.

Finance stops his clicking and recovers his tongue.

'How much is it supposed to cost?' he asks.

'A couple of million,' you reply with a gleam of triumph in your eyes. 'But that wasn't before I did some fairly tough bargaining. I brought 'em down a whack, I can tell you. It was rough going there for a while, but I showed 'em that Amalgamated Matchbox wasn't a bottomless pit of the old shekels. I think we struck a pretty fair bargain.'

Murmurs of 'Well done me boy,' 'That's the spirit,' 'Done the founder proud lad' etc. from the board.

'You mean that you've signed a contract for two million?' asks Finance, his voice dry, like the desert sand.

'I certainly did, Finance. The old John Henry on the dotted line, and all that. Took 'em at their word while the iron was hot. They can't back out now.'

'Neither can we,' says Engineering. 'And that two million will be six before we've anything to show for it.' He takes out his slide rule and starts to slide it back and forth.

'Put that damn thing away man, this is serious,' cuts in Finance. 'Whether it's two or six it isn't on the budget, and frankly I don't see where the money's coming from.'

'Out of the savings, gentlemen. That's what it's for.' You look wildly round for support. Time for your trump card. 'I've thought of everything,' you say with a chuckle. 'We've financed the whole deal. The manufacturer owns a leasing company. Dead simple. We buy it from their manufacturing division, and then sell it to their leasing division who leases it back to us.'

'Sounds unnecessarily complicated to me,' says Finance. 'But that only takes care of the equipment itself. What about the effort that each of the departments is going to have to make to get it to work?'

'Well, as I said before, these technical details I leave up to you. I'm only giving you the tools, as someone once said. I decided that we'd never get anywhere just talking. We needed some action. A catalyst, if you like, to get you chaps moving. We'd reached a point where any decision was better than no decision. And, after all, it's my job to step in when you chaps can't agree.' Text book stuff. Difficult to argue with.

'You don't have to mess about with pennies in the slot with electricity,' interrupts the Colonel. 'No one can ever find a penny when it's needed, and the lights get so dim you can't even see to read your accounts receivable.'

'You're quite right Colonel,' shouts Finance. 'It'll be megabucks in the slot from now on.'

'Mega what?' asks the Colonel.

'Bucks,' shouts Finance. 'Megabucks. We've had a change of currency since the turn of the century.'

'I warned 'em this would happen if they put the sovereign out of circulation. But if you don't have gas, at least you don't have to mess about changing the size of the slot.'

'If I may interrupt the Colonel, J.B., I'd like to know who we've bought this computer from,' says Marketing.

'Sorry, I forgot to mention the lucky winner of the competition. It's the Hairy Hardware Company. You've probably heard of them.' This revelation surely can't be so controversial.

'That was a smart move, J.B.,' groans Engineering. 'They haven't a single installation in our branch.'

'That was exactly my point,' you counter in triumph. 'Part of the entry fee was a substantial reduction in the price. Do a good job, and our word will be worth a fortune, I told 'em.'

'Tell us about the competition you held J.B.,' says Marketing. 'If you bothered to hold one.'

'We don't want to waste the time of our busy board members going into technical details, so we can take this up later if it's of any real interest. Very briefly I worked out a list of questions which I gave to the various manufacturers, and simply awarded the contract to the chap with the best answers. The traditional way we do things here at A.M. Had 'em meet me at the club of course. Gave each of 'em a whole afternoon of my time. A good half dozen altogether.'

'What questions?' asks Marketing.

'Some pretty searching ones, if you must know,' you reply. 'What equipment do you have? How fast does it run? What sort of prices do you try to charge? How much are you prepared to come down to get in on our kind of business? How soon can you deliver? And so on. Straight from the shoulder. Really pinned 'em down. And I got some pretty fascinating answers. Did you realise gentlemen that we're up against the speed of light? That's moving right along, you know. We can't afford to pass up an opportunity like this.' You lean back and beam across at the board.

'Gas light or electric light?' asks the Colonel.

'Did you ask about the software?' asks Engineering.

'Support?' asks Quality Control.

'Standard packages?' asks Finance.

'Training?' asks Marketing. You stop beaming.

'Hold on, hold on gentlemen. There's no need to be abusive,' you react. 'I'm sure that all these things can be taken care of by Hairy.' And this is the point where you blind them with science. 'I'll have you know that they've got the most flexible front end in the business. It won't be necessary for me to bring you their Managing Director's head on a platter. We're dealing with businessmen of the old school here you know. They're not going to let us down.'

'Which old school, J.B.?' asks Marketing. 'Who was the salesman?'

You cough and adjust your tie. 'Well as a matter of fact it was the wife's nephew who actually landed the deal. But mark you,' you hasten to add, 'family connections had nothing to do with it. You know I'm no believer in mixing family with business.'

Silence.

'And it doesn't leak out in the air like gas.' The Colonel is back at the attack.

'Thank you, Colonel.' It's wonderful to have the solid backing of the board at times like this. 'And thank you all gentlemen for your time and involvement. We shall give this matter our full attention and will report progress.'

The meeting breaks up and the two groups go their separate ways. Congratulations boss, you've at last succeeded in doing something that you've been trying to do ever since you took over the reigns of Amalgamated Matchbox. You have united your departmental managers. You have given them a common bond. An invader from outer space. But is it you, or should the computer itself take the credit?

4 Sources of profit

It didn't start the way you wanted it. Your motives were honourable, but you jumped the gun. It was clear from the reaction of your department heads that there was a great deal to be done before signing any dotted line, but it took a desperate action on your part to find that out. Fortunately it was only a bad dream. You haven't really signed anything, so the way is clear to do the thing properly.

Where do we start then? Well, where does the company start? Why not now forget all the stuff you've seen in the ads and only half understood, if at all, about integrated this, compatible that and instantaneous the other? Concentrate your gaze instead on your own company; look for nuggets of lost profit that are lying there waiting to be picked up. It is the quest for profit that should be your guiding light in the computing effort, and fundamental to it is the Inverse Law of Profitability:

$$\text{PROFITABILITY} = \frac{1}{\text{FORMALITY}}$$

the explanation of which will unfold itself during the course of the chapter.

The obstacle in your path is not your lack of knowledge of computers, but your intimate familiarity with the mess around you. This is known as the Instamatic syndrome. On vacation, when you arrive at a new, exotic paradise, you are flooded with impressions and you shoot your Instamatic wildly in all directions. You use up half your film on the first day, a quarter on the second, and you bring home the last quarter unused, and have to take the annual pictures of the cat and grandma to finish up the roll.

The human brain soon reaches saturation point, familiarity takes over, and we carefully step over the empties instead of returning them to the shop.

Your first impressions of Amalgamated Matchbox were of the mail room, and that was forty years ago. You swore at the time that if you ever rose to be chief sorter you'd revolutionise

. . . . if you ever rose to be chief sorter you'd revolutionise the place.

the place. Unfortunately you were promoted diagonally to Knot Inspection and you haven't seen the mail room since. Consequently it hasn't changed a lot.

Somehow you have to overcome the Instamatic syndrome, and perhaps the best way of doing this is to borrow a younger pair of eyes from some far-off place for a limited period of time and for an agreed sum. However you do it, the place to start looking is at the forefront of the organisation, the point of sale or the area of service. Everything else you do is a consequence of the success of the man who deals with the customers (or the patients or the appliers for permission to modify their frontage).

Assuming for the moment that your company is in the business of selling physical objects, then all your salesman needs are infinitely long shelves of every conceivable variety of object you make, available for instant delivery. Give him that and you'll never see hide nor hair of him. But the classical struggle in your company is a three-cornered affair between Sales, Manufacturing and Accounting. Manufacturing likes to have long-life, uninterrupted production of identical objects, while Accounting wants to keep the shelves empty to avoid tying up capital in stock. Thus the dashing of the salesman's hopes and the cost of the gap between promise and delivery. But not all is lost thanks to Washington's Law (he didn't have a forest of cherry trees): The next best thing to infinity is accuracy. While infinity, if you could have it, would make the job of selling effortless, accuracy at least enables you to be honest and reliable. The trouble is that traditionally the salesman rarely has an accurate picture of the contents of the warehouse, and has to substitute with a universal crossing of the fingers.

So your first question is, can I now provide the salesman with an accurate picture? Can I create some sort of systematic method of telling him precisely what he can sell at this precise moment; what alternatives he has; if it isn't there now when it will be; current prices; delivery time and so on? While twenty years ago the answer to this question was mostly no, it is now mostly yes. Because there is now such a wide variety of systematic order-entry methods and experience available, the probability must be high that you too can climb on the wagon.

You kill two flies with this first swat, you provide operative accuracy which improves your competitive position, and you provide the basis for tighter inventory control and a consequent freeing up of capital. The latter is directly measurable and can mean reductions of ten to twenty per cent, and this should more than pay the cost of the new system. The value of knowing precisely what you are doing is never fully measurable, but part of its value can be seen with time as sales curves bend upwards. If they don't, something is wrong and you have a job to do. But that will be three years from now, and when you dig into the details you will learn something profound and valuable.

But that isn't all. The provision of a currently accurate picture necessarily implies using the apparatus involved to make the actual order. This leads immediately to automatic instruction-printing in the warehouses. Two more flies, speeded up shipping and reduced errors. And the automatic collection of the day's transactions becomes the input to the nightly production of bills and other bureaucratic consequences. A whole swarm.

To complete the picture, all entries to stock have to be registered the moment they arrive.

But that's more than enough to start with. Let us call the whole thing the Sales System and illustrate it with a simple picture, Figure 4.1

Now the first step to take in acquiring yourself a sales system is to convince the salesman. Don't imagine that somehow you can create it without him, and don't try to commit the managerial crime of Vertical Imposition, forcing it on him from above. He will violently object. Be prepared for that. Firstly he won't have any belief in anything newfangled. Secondly he's too busy selling. Any effort on his part taken off the job will mean a reduction in company business. This is part of the cost, not to be omitted from the balance sheet. The company has no option but slow down for a while. So be a tiger and stand still before you spring.

This book is about influencing and steering the computer people, but you have no hope of doing this all by yourself. Your task is limited to ensuring that your company as a whole manages them, and to get your department managers on your side you pick them off one by one, starting with the toughest nut, the salesman. But how?

My advice is, use the Balchen Japanese technique. The Norwegian professor, J.G. Balchen, spent a whole decade

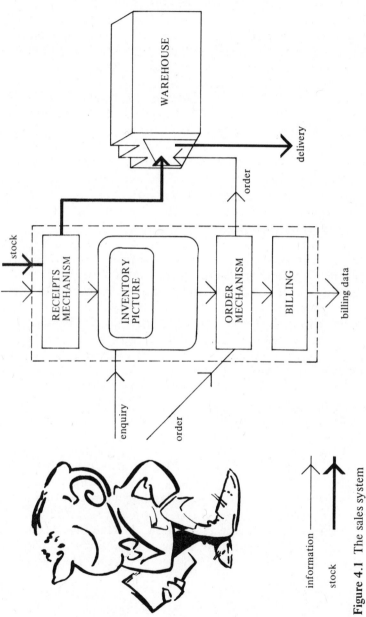

Figure 4.1 The sales system

information ———→

stock ⟹

trying to convince the ship owners to install computers on board. Finally he hit on the idea of having a friend tell his next door neighbour, a prominent ship owner, that the Japanese were already doing it. The result was that Norwegian shipping was the first to use on-board computers.

All Japanese companies use computer-based sales systems.

Having roped in your salesman, you now confine your efforts to producing a sales system. In the meantime you ignore all appeals for any other use of a computer. If you spread your attention and your energy over too broad a scope, nothing of any substance will get done. Of course, you may already be doing things with a computer. Most people are these days. If so, ignore it, i.e. delegate it. You can pick this up and deal with it appropriately when the time is ripe. Or your successor can.

A word about the inventory. This, of course, can be many things. It might be heaps of pipes and flanges in a warehouse. It might be the contents of the shelves of a supermarket, the output from a power plant, the contents of petroleum tanks, or wagons on a railway network. It might be housed in a single structure, or a network of structures spread around the country. On the other hand it might be an 'imaginary' inventory, for example the policies of an insurance company (infinite in number), or the money in a bank (apparently infinite). Different types of inventory have different types of problem associated with them, and different types of solution. It must not be inferred that there is in any way a standard inventory control system. Far from it.

When the sales system is up and running, and you and the salesman are in firm control of the computer, you then turn your attention to the next system. To which direction should you turn? What are the options? Well, again, what do you do? Do you manufacture the objects? Do you buy them? Do you subcontract part of the production? Are the objects large or complicated? Do you have a large engineering staff? Do you have a high incidence of engineering change? Do you have a sizeable proportion of your capital tied up in unpaid bills? Do you send the stuff out haphazardly, wasting time and fuel? There are a lot of questions, but one of them will probably

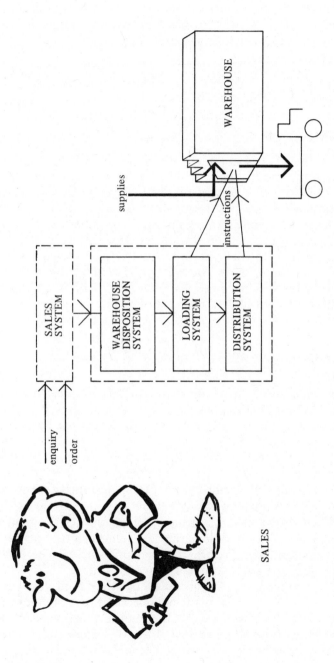

Figure 4.2 The delivery system

lead to a lost-profit target which is either larger or more accessable than any of the others. That, then, is the direction to go.

Let us take a look at some of the options to give you an idea of what to look for.

Delivery

Why are your warehouses where they are? Because your grandfather put them there? Would you put them there yourself today if you were starting now? How would you decide where to put them? Do you know how costly or profitable each one is? Do you even know what they contain, with any accuracy? How do you decide which one shall supply each order? How are the orders delivered? How much needless time and fuel are you wasting? Do you really need that many trucks, ships, pipelines or bicycles? And so on. A good delivery system can unlock a lot of profit.

Manufacture

Do you manufacture your own stuff? If so you have a gold mine of possibilities because it is in the factory where a substantial amount of computer pioneering has been done. There exist a lot of well worked-out techniques, but, more importantly, there is now a great deal of equipment available to the factory that can be tied into the computer. We shall take a look at this equipment in Chapter 6, and shall confine ourselves at this point to the techniques.

What does a manufacturing order in your company mean? The assembly of a wide variety of components? The setting of jigs and manufacture of tools and dies? The careful scheduling of work through the various shops?

How skilled are your people? Do they need detailed instructions? Can you vary the detail easily? Do you know how far down the learning curve they are for each product? Do you know how effective your training schemes are?

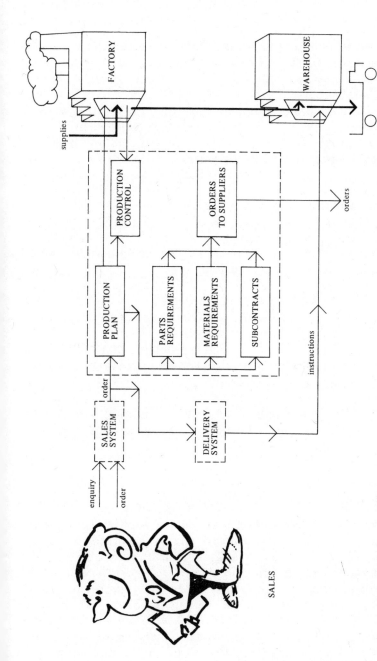

Figure 4.3 The manufacturing system

How complicated are the parts you make? How accurate must they be? Is it conceivable that computer control of one sort or another could do the work more quickly or more accurately?

How accurate a picture do you have of the work in progress? Where are the bottlenecks? How frequently do the same bottlenecks crop up? How close is reality to plan? Are your planning methods adequate?

How often do you receive design changes from Engineering? How do you implement them? How do you keep tabs on the various versions?

How does Engineering release new design? How straightforward is the task of implementing new design? How large a liaison staff do you employ to iron out the misunderstandings? Well these are a few questions to get you started. Naturally your chief of manufacturing will have been asking these and many others daily ever since you landed him with the job, but what have you done about it? Again, you are going to have to pull him off the job to get any action, but you now have an ally, the salesman. One of the problems that the salesman has is unfulfilled promises based on Manufacturing's forecasts. The salesman always subtracts, he never adds to delivery times. He was born that way. So it is in his interests too that the factory is a tighter ship. And in addition, don't forget, you have all those Japanese factories humming away in competition.

Design

Our last set of questions backs us naturally into the design stage. Again, a great deal has already been achieved in the engineering profession, and one can usefully ask questions of the following sort.

How long is your design cycle? How cumbersome is it? How many square miles of floor space do you take up drawing lines on sheets of paper? How accurate are these lines? How much time is spent drawing them in the first place? Then in measuring them afterwards? And how often do you

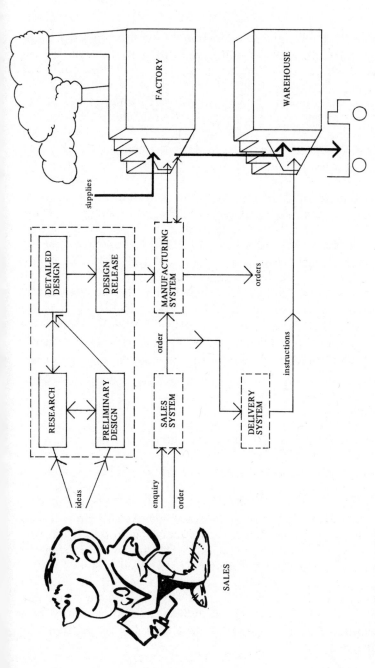

Figure 4.4 The design system

do that? How much time making your drawings artistic or even neat? How much unnecessary drawing do you do? Do you draw to impart information or because you enjoy the therapy?

How much time to you spend performing calculations? How often do you make errors? What do these cost in delay and rework?

How often do you send in design changes? Who decides? How necessary are they? Are you aware of their impact on the production line?

Again, enough questions to get you started. And again, questions that the chief engineer has been asking for years. If you decide to attack Engineering after Manufacturing you already have allies in Sales and Manufacturing (as well as the Japanese engineering profession), but it could be economically arguable to go for Engineering first. If so, the salesman is still a good ally since it is he who has the loudest voice in all decisions of what should be made. If Engineering can shorten their design time and provide Manufacturing with better input, the salesman gets his new gadgets out on the market earlier.

Purchasing

Even if you have a factory the chances are that you order things from the outside world, either from other people's shelves or according to your own design. This gives rise to the following typical questions. How well has the sub-contractor followed your design intent? What is the quality like? How many should you test of each batch? How do you ensure that the correct tests are made? Who sells what? Are you exploiting the competition? Or do you buy from old reliable friends? Has the stuff been delivered on time? What's the hold up? What are the delays costing in terms of held-up production? You are always vulnerable when you sub-contract. How can you reduce this vulnerability to a minimum? Again, there is usually a lot of profit to be squeezed out.

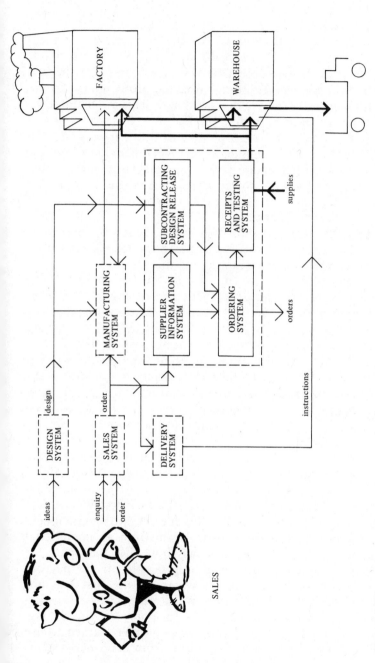

Figure 4.5 The purchasing system

We have gone far enough for the moment, and it might help to focus our thinking by drawing some more simple pictures. Let us suppose that we have found that the best sequence of implementation, from the profit point of view, is the sequence we have discussed here. This is illustrated by building each picture from its predecessor. (Figures 4.2 to 4.5.)

At this point we have a picture with few loose ends, and it looks deceptively simple. If you work backwards and expand each dotted square you begin to have something that would cover the wall, however what is more pertinent is that already you have at least a decade of work ahead of you – if you do things properly.

We shall return later to such questions as how this can be carried out, what it might cost, how to organise and plan. But the hope is that somewhere in this set of pictures lies at least one source of profit, lost in the hurlyburly of the operations of your company, that could be dug out by means of a good system under the control of the operational boss.

In addition to the *operational* systems are the *support* and *control* systems, budgeting, accounting, costing, payroll, personnel, and so on. The ultimate output from the operational systems is of course the bills, but in addition to that is the recording of time and expense incurred throughout these departments. A comprehensive picture of systems to cope with that is really something in three dimensions, which we won't attempt to draw.

However there is a profound difference between the operational systems and the support systems. Historically it is the latter that have come first but it is the former that produce the savings. Most organisations today have the accounts on the computer, but this doesn't save much money, particularly if it is done in isolation from an operational system. Very few companies can show that they paid for their computer in terms of getting people off the payroll. The reason why the support systems came first was not economics but understanding. We already had well understood, well developed procedures for doing the accounting. And a computer is a *procedure machine.* We learned to use the computer by lifting the accounts from the paper systems or punched-card systems, often making no change whatsoever in the procedures.

The problem with the operational systems is that we have to create procedures. Either we have to modify existing ones, or, more commonly, we have to create procedures for the first time. And this is' not easy. A lot of feeling may be involved. Accounting is clear-cut, inventory-control isn't. It takes time and it costs money even to get to the starting line with operational systems. Hence the Inverse Law of Profitability cited at the start of the chapter: the more you are already formalised and proceduralised the less hope you have of improving what you are doing and increasing your profit. On the other hand, the more you operate by hunch, individual initiative, and muddling through, the greater the probability of nuggets of lost profit waiting to be dug out by a modicum of organisation.

Had we not had a base of well understood procedures ready to put on the computer in the 1950s, we may well never have had computers for commercial use. The argument, the delay and the cost of creating procedures would have drowned all hope of success, and hence the money to pay for computer development. This discussion is continued in Chapter 9 in which we shall discuss some concrete techniques.

5 *Almost all you need to know about the computer itself*

The automatic stored-program electronic digital computer, to give it its full title, has been enshrouded in what sounds like gobbeldegook ever since its birth in 1949. And this has been one of the troubles. The combination of its essential invisibility and the lack of concern on the part of the priest-hood to create and explain a terminology comprehensible to the outsider has made it very difficult for the would-be user to get what he might want, if only he knew that he wanted it. I have always found this difficult to understand, because if the industry made its wares more appetising it would presumably sell more of them. But I suppose the explanation if that computer people understand one another comfortably enough, so they don't know what your problem is.

On the other hand you can't just sit back and expect to be spoon-fed. You must make some effort to understand computing just as you have to understand things like Mercator's projection, double-entry bookkeeping, radio-carbon dating, glaciation and DNA. By now they are part of our culture, like it or not, and there's no reason to make a special exception, especially when you come to realise how childishly simple they are. It's much easier to learn how a computer works than to understand how Michael Ventris managed to translate Linear B. And the essence of control-ling anything is understanding the thing you are trying to control. So this is the short course on understanding the computer.

The computer consists of four things (the motor car 400

and the airplane 40,000!): a device for storing numbers, a device for doing simple arithmetic on them, a means of getting numbers in and out of the device, and a means of controlling what happens. It couldn't be much simpler, and it won't get much more complicated as we take a closer look at each.

The device for storing numbers is just like a pad of paper, but it happens to be electronic because it has to operate very quickly. We call it the *memory* of the computer, but it bears no similarity whatsoever to the human memory. Indeed it could hardly be more different.

Moreover the pad is of *squared* electronic paper, and each square is called either a *memory location, word* or *byte*, and in each we can place a number. There is no practical limit to the magnitude of a number that can be placed in the memory, provided we use enough squares. Astronomers are interested in extremely large numbers, but they have no more difficulty in using the computer than the payroll man, who is interested in very small ones.

The fact that the memory is electronic means not only that access to numbers is very fast, but that they can easily be changed. It's as though we did arithmetic on a sheet of paper using an eraser which didn't leave a mark. We re-use the 'paper' all the time because we don't have an infinite supply, even though we may have a lot of it.

As to size, in 1950 a computer memory consisted of about 1000 locations. By 1960 it had grown to about 30,000, since when it has continued to grow steadily to several million. We talk about memory size in units of 1000 to which we assign the letter K. Thus a 64K byte memory is simply a memory consisting of 64,000 bytes.

Device number two is called the *arithmetic unit*. It has the capability of containing a number and adding it to any number already placed in the memory, or subtracting it, multiplying or dividing it. But division requires the ability to take care of a remainder, so actually the arithmetic unit has to be able to contain two numbers. And it can store either of these numbers in any location in the memory, as many times as we like.

So a computer is nothing but a very fast arithmetic machine attached to a large supply of numbers. It cannot do advanced mathematics. If you want to do advanced mathematics you have to fool it; you have to replace the continuous with the discrete. You have to approximate the infinitesimal with the very small but finite. But provided you approximate closely enough the answers will be good enough. In banking, insurance and in your accounting programs the results are always exact. These things only require arithmetic. But in engineering and science results are usually inexact. Engineers work to a tolerance anyway, so provided the tolerance of the computer is no worse than their ability to draw and measure, and the ability of the factory to cut, everything's OK.

The third type of device is the ability to get numbers in and out of the memory: *input—output.* In the early days input was made by means of punched cards and punched paper tape, two devices that were ready to hand from older technologies. While output was achieved by means of a printer. Later on other kinds of device were hooked on to the computer, but we shall introduce these later in this chapter, and devote the whole of the next chapter to them.

The fourth aspect of the computer is the business of controlling it, telling it what to do. This is achieved by means of something called a *program.* And this is where things start getting metaphysical, because a program isn't an object, and takes a variety of physical forms. But before we get into that it might be worth looking at some other kinds of program. The series of events on the TV is called a programme, but a computer program bears little resemblance to it. If we think of a washing machine programme we come a little closer. A washing machine programme consists of a series of instructions to various parts of the machine to do things at various points in time. Turn on hot water. Roll the barrel. Squirt in some soap. Wait a while. Turn off hot water. Let the water out. And so on.

If you know nothing more about a computer than we've already said, you still wouldn't have much trouble in dreaming up a way of programming it. You wouldn't be wanting it to turn water on and off, but you would want it to add numbers.

You would want a program to consist of such instructions as add this number, subtract that number, save this result, read this card, print that answer. We're getting there already, but which 'this' or 'that'? How could we identify the numbers we're dealing with? In the washing machine we have very few objects to deal with. Cold tap, hot tap, low-speed drive, spin drive, soap-squirter, pump, air heater, fan. That's about it. But the computer memory may consist of thousands or millions of locations or bytes. How do we identify them? The answer is that we provide each one with an *address,* much like the address of a house in a street; independent of its contents. Contiguous locations in memory are assigned consecutive digital numbers as addresses, 0, 1, 2 . . . 10,000, and higher. So a piece of program might look something like this:

> Put the number in location 99 in the Arithmetic Unit.
> Add ”   ”   ”   ”   502 to it.
> Subtract ”   ”   ”   743 from it.
> Store the result in location 100.

And would be written like this:

> PUT   99
> ADD   502
> SUB   743
> STORE   100

That's easier to understand than how a carburettor works. If location 99 contained a five, 502 a seven, 743 a two, what would end up in location 100? I make it a ten.

Now how about where the program is while it is in control of the computer? Where is the TV program? Well it's in several places, in the newspaper, in the minds of the viewers and the ulcer of the producer, but it's *not* in the TV. The TV contains electronics but it doesn't contain the program. Where is the washing machine programme though? Again we're getting closer. It's in the washing machine. It's not in amongst the dirty clothes, but it is inside the outer cover. How about the computer? What's the essential difference between the two? Well the program in the former is only concerned with washing clothes, and it does the same thing every time with the possible exception of where it starts and hence how much hell it beats out of the clothes. A computer program, on the other hand, may be set up to do all sorts of different things: display the contents of an account number, compute the stresses in a bridge, issue an airline ticket.

Enough clues. It must be obvious by now that the program must be put inside the computer, and must be put where it can easily be changed, i.e. in the memory. There's no other possibility. We want to be able to put all sorts of different programs into the computer at different times of the day. The computer is a quick-change artist, and it's the memory that makes it possible.

But wait, you cry, the memory only contains numbers. How can it contain instructions? Well the right-hand half of an instruction is a number already, and what's stopping us setting up a numerical coding system for the left-hand half? We could say that ADD was assigned the code number 1, SUBTRACT 2, PUT 3, STORE 4, and so on. So our little bit of program would be written:

3	99
1	502
2	743
4	100

That's solved the problem, and the only question left is *how* do we put the program in the memory? But what's the problem? What's the simplest thing we could do? Why not just regard each instruction as a simple number and put it in a single location? But then we need a rule. Let us agree to construct our computer in a way such that a *sequence* of instructions is placed in a *sequence* of locations. Again, it's the simplest arrangement you could think of. Let's do it. Let's place 399 in location 1001, for example. Then 1502 goes in 1002, and so on, so that our program now looks like this:

Location	Instruction
1001	399
1002	1502
1003	2743
1004	4100

And when the program is fully loaded we tell the computer to start by taking control to the first instruction (in location 800 for example). When it has carried out this instruction it takes the next from 801, then from 802 and so on, one instruction at a time until the program has finished. Then we can load a new program where the old one was sitting.

It's still simpler than the carburettor, and a lot simpler than learning German. And that's all there is to it, except for a few onion-like layers wrapped around it. But these are also important to understand so we'll carry on for a while.

That's precisely what the computer consisted of in the early fifties, but it began to evolve in complexity as the result of a series of solutions to a series of problems. When the computer first began to work it was such a vast improvement over what we had before, desk calculators and punched card equipment, that we were more than satisfied with it. Well, if only it were a bit more reliable we wouldn't have to keep getting up in the middle of the night to get our five minutes. But that was only a minor gripe.

But the human spirit is a restless object, and what started out as a source of heady adventure and excitement, the act of writing computer programs, after a while started to become a tedious chore. As only those who have done it know, computer programming is a really exciting occupation. Why this should be could probably be the subject of an entire book, so I daren't attempt an explanation in these pages. But, for whatever the reason, the act of going from an idea to a correct result is tremendous fun. However, as with writing a symphony it is not without its tedious aspects, and often the journey from idea to result can be a long one. And the journey may have nothing to do with the logic or the philosophy of the idea, which may be all very sound. The problems lie in the arbitrary details of the computer which really get in the way. If we're honest about it, a great deal of the satisfaction we got in the early days was derived from solving problems created *by* the computer itself rather than solving problems *using* the computer. We solved problems very often despite and not because of the design of the machine.

The basic problem was having to *think* like a computer in order to write a program. We had to break the problem down into a very large number of microscopic steps (add this, subtract that, multiply it by the other), write each step down, and get it right. Not a single error was tolerated. One mistake and the entire program was wrong. This was something new in the history of mankind. Until now the world around us was, to a greater or lesser extent, tolerant. No one was expected to be perfect. Generals lose battles and still get their pensions. Schoolmasters are stumped by the class genius and only get laughed at. The mounties don't always get their man. And engineers do all their work to within an allowable tolerance. But not the computer programmer. The computer did what you told it, not what you thought you told it, and this requirement for precision became a great consumer of time, precisely the problem the computer was supposed to solve.

The business, firstly of describing the entire journey in simple steps, then of winkling out all the wrong ones, was very time-consuming, and although the computer was fast when you got there, getting there took more time than people could eventually tolerate.

Why think and write like a computer? Why not use the computer itself to help you think and write like a human being? Of all the problems that you could take to the computer, why not take the one that's closest to your nose? Programming. Why not think and write in a way that comes naturally to you and have a program convert the result into steps and language of the computer?

Language? What's this got to do with language? Well, to be honest, it's not much of a language, but you must admit ADD is a verb, while 99 could be regarded as a noun. This being so an instruction is a sentence, albeit a very short one. So that we can say that a program is a long series of sentences couched in the language that the designer has breathed into the computer. And the task before us in the mid-fifties was to create languages that would make it much easier, and therefore quicker and cheaper, to get computer programs up and running. And having constructed a 'user' language a program was written which would translate sentences in the user language into instructions in the computer language. Such a translator is called a *compiler,* a very important step in the development of computer technology. Compilers are normally supplied by the manufacturer along with the hardware.

A very large number of languages has been spawned, but most of the world's programming is undertaken in very few, and most of these were developed in a very short, explosive period between 1958 and 1962. It would be beyond the scope of this book to consider these languages in any detail, however there are two facts that must be clearly understood, firstly that these higher-level languages, as they are called, have given us a gain in programmer productivity of at least ten to one, and even as much as a hundred to one. So without them there wouldn't have been enough people available to handle the computers that have been produced, i.e. computers would have been prohibitively expensive. And secondly that languages differ enormously in the kinds of computation they can handle. You can express more or less the same sentiments in English, Russian or Chinese, but (to take some programming languages without saying what they are for) you haven't a hope of translating between APT, COBOL and MARY. So it is the task of management to ensure that the technical staff have the appropriate languages for their work, manifest in the appropriate compilers.

The second problem that wasn't obvious on day one of the age of computers was that of operating the machine. You wrote your program, you rushed into the computing room, joined the queue, grabbed the console, pressed a button or two, lit a cigarette, and after a while staggered off with a pile of paper, shaking your head in bewilderment. It was easy then because the number of users was small, and computer time wasn't at a premium. But when the number of users grew from tens to thousands, queues in the machine room were unthinkable, and we couldn't tolerate the time wasted between runs.

Again, why not write a computer program which could handle a queue of jobs automatically? And hire a new specimen of humanity called a professional operator whose job it was to handle the physical queue? Again 1958 was the year when this all started and again by about 1962 most computers were operated in this manner. Such a program was called variously an *automatic operating system, monitor* or *executive.*

Since that time, in distinction to a stagnation in the development of languages, operating systems have developed out of all recognition and have taken over more and more of the chores of computing, not only operating but programming, writing, editing, checkout, filing, as well as handling the ever-growing array of gadgets that we can hang on the computer and which we shall be discussing in the next chapter.

The next of the unforeseen problems was that of the sheer magnitude of data that computers would be called upon to handle. The only thought at the beginning was to make arithmetic automatic and fast. But you would argue immediately that this necessarily implies larger quantities of numbers.

It's meaningless to try to do high-speed arithmetic on only a few numbers. Nevertheless the first computer memories were (by today's standards) very small, and it took a year or two before they were supported by any kind of extension. What was needed was an automatic equivalent of books, catalogues etc., which are extensions of the human memory. The first of these was really right around the corner. As luck would have it, *magnetic tape* had already been developed as an audio device, and it did not require much ingenuity to adapt it as a numerical device. Thus magnetism replaced paper for cheap, large-scale storage of numbers. Magnetic tape was followed by *magnetic drum* and *disc* which were more expensive but allowed a much faster access to data than tape, and therefore increased the actual running speed of a program.

As to speed, we normally talk in terms of *cycle time,* the time taken to add two numbers together, anthropo-morphically equivalent to the human heart beat. The early computers had cycle times of several milliseconds, while today's have cycle times of less than a microsecond (a millionth of a second).

So we see the basic idea of the computer surrounded by unavoidable layers of detailed technology, both in terms of hardware and programs, but if you understand the reasons for this technology, none of it is difficult to understand. By way of definition we can discern three distinct levels. Firstly the stuff that hurts you if it falls on your foot, the *hardware.* Secondly, the array of programs that enable you to use the hardware easily, the compilers, operating system, etc., which we can usefully call the *software;* and thirdly the actual productive uses of the computer, the applications programs. As to who provides what, most of the software is provided by the manufacturers along with the hardware, but most of the applications programs you create yourself, although you can buy them ready made if you are lucky enough to find ones suited to your business.

In Chapter 7 we shall introduce a few more terms con-cerned with the way we actually run programs on the com-puter. In the early days there were no options, we brought a program to the computer, ran it, and removed it. This we call *batch* processing. But today we can keep it there all the time and run it whenever we want to, perhaps thousands of times a day. This type of operation bears the unfortunate label *real time.* However real time has a wide variety of flavours which has a great bearing on the economics of a program, therefore we shall postpone this discussion until then.

One of the purposes in explaining all this is that although today's computer is simple in principle, it is very complicated in detail, and the task of obtaining the right amounts of hardware and software, and tuning these to your workload is not easy. In the early days a computer had fewer options than a motor car. It was a model T except for the colour. But today it's almost nothing but options, both in nature and extent. No two computers look alike any more. And the question that you must hammer away at until you are satisfied with the answer is, do we have all the right options to get our job done? In particular do we have enough central memory to house all the software and still get the productive work done? And this problem raises its ugly head in the question of the contract. What is a computer contract? What should it specify? What should it guarantee? Who is responsible for what? What happens if it isn't up to snuff? A computer contract is not something you can delegate at the point of signing. If you are going to use the computer properly, by definition it is going to affect the economics of your organisation. A bad contract can sabotage those economics, and you could even find yourself without a company, as we shall see in Chapter 19.

This chapter didn't contain all you need to know about the computer because you have no option but dig into some of the details of the particular computer you happen to have or plan to order. But it contained the necessary basics, to be followed by a few nuances later in the book.

6 Getting your hands on it

As we have said, *ad nauseam,* the computer is invisible. But this is not true of the equipment that we hang on it, which is the subject of this chapter. A proper appreciation of the kinds of equipment available today that can be used in the office, factory, laboratory, ward, counter, ship and so on, will give you an excellent measure of control over the system and its perpetrators, as well as enabling you to use the computer properly.

Throughout most of history the obtaining and distribution of water has been a fairly simple business.

But first let us consider a relevant analogy, that of the delivery of the commodity water. Throughout most of history the obtaining and distribution of water has been a fairly simple business. In most cultures people dug wells and surrounded them with walls and steps, they built their dwellings alongside and manufactured pots with which the ladies were permitted to transport the stuff to their dwellings. An improvement in the system usually meant an enlarging of the well, the construction of lighter or more robust pots or a stronger rail to clutch when climbing the steps.

But in modern times we have discovered the existence of the physical phenomenon of pressure, which has led to a revolution in the use of water. At the receiving end of the pipe we arranged for it to come out of taps in the kitchen, showers in the bathroom, hoses in the garage, sprinklers in the garden, and sprays on the dentist's drill. We take its existence for granted and it is generations since any city dweller saw a well. Our sole concern is the ease with which we can bring water to bear on the object to be filled or wetted, and our only problems are burst pipes.

Moreover, the number of taps, hosepipes etc., coupled with statistical knowledge of their use, creates the requirement for the size of the well. And as cities mushroom, anonymous planners in the depth of their halls provide new wells, but these activities are of no interest at all to the tap turner − unless, of course, the tap does nothing but give out a gurgling noise. The analogous aim in using the computer is to create devices that fit harmoniously into the application landscape; devices that can be turned on and off easily by the people around, without any thought of what is going on in the pipes or the information well situated in some far-off building; devices that are appropriate to the task, and therefore to a large extent specialised for the use of particular people working in a particular place in a particular way.

Perhaps the most fundamental pieces of information that a computer system needs are space and time. In other words, it needs to know where every device is, and what the time is. And it is very easy to provide for this. Each device, whatever its nature, can have an *address,* a number attached to it as unique as the number on the door of your house. And every computer has a built-in clock so that it can either register the time that something occurred, or can cause something to occur at a particular time.

In addition to space and time are such attributes as who, how, what, how much, how often and so forth, and it is these that provide the basic differences between the devices.

Now one of the obstacles to getting managers to want to understand computing is that they know beforehand that they are fiendishly complicated. Well a city water supply probably has some rather complicated aspects to it, but the kitchen tap is simple enough. And there are some extremely simple and cheap devices that can be hung on the computer. Similarly, even though it is possible to have the computer carry out extremely complicated mathematical computations, there are some very profitable examples of having it repeatedly add the number one and print out the answer. Computers don't have to do complicated things to be useful.

The simplest kind of device that we could possibly think of could consist of a single, simple indicator, a lamp or needle. Such a device could be used to interrogate the computer to ask a simple question which admitted of two answers, yes or no. For example, if the device were attached to the bed of a patient in hospital it could be used to ask whether or not the patient was due to have the standard meal of the day. A steady light might mean yes, and a blinking light, no. I do not know that a device as simple as this has actually been constructed, but it would be a simple enough matter. Furthermore the simplest device in common use is not much more complicated. It consists of a small metal box into which one can insert a plastic badge containing a few holes, or a magnetisable strip. We call this box a badge-reader, and in the badge we may encode a man's number, a part number, a job number or whatever, and may scatter such devices around the factory to register clocking in and out, the movement of parts or tools, the time spent by whom, on what jobs etc. The important advantage of such a simple device is its ease of use, and the practical impossibility of error. There is nothing to do other than pop the badge into the slot. But the main disadvantage is that it is impossible to add any other information than that contained in the badge, plus the time of day and the physical location of the reader.

To enable a wider range of information to pass to and fro it is necessary for a device to have a number of buttons for input and a number of lights or printed characters as output. A device of this sort which still retains some of the error-prevention aspects of the badge-reader is the airline terminal used by SAS. There the information, rather than being punched in a badge, is printed on a plastic card which is placed on top of the device. The information consists of flight numbers and to ascertain whether a seat is available, the operator pushes a button immediately above the required number, and another to the immediate right. The computer replies with a green light if a seat is available, or a red one if it isn't. Still extremely simple to use.

The next step is to make available a larger set of keys and the ability to print a character for each key. For example the keys of a typewriter, printing on paper or on the face of a TV screen. In this case the information that flows back and forth consists of words and numbers, often in full linguistic sentences. This implies an infinitely wide range of possibilities of use. However the possibility for error is correspondingly great, and the computer must be on the watch-out for nonsense, and must be able to tell the user every time it is possible or even obvious that the user has done something wrong. On the other hand, the computer can lead the user along, telling him what to do next. So it is not a major task to teach people to use such devices. We can build a great deal of teaching into the process itself.

If we don't need immediate contact with the computer (something that costs money), we can instead arrange for the keys to print characters on paper which can be read directly by the computer without the necessity of keying into cards or magnetic tape. Such characters can be of special type fonts, or printed in 'magnetic' ink. We call these facilities Optical Character Recognition (OCR) and Magnetic Ink Character Recognition (MICR).

Although everything in the computer is represented in terms of numbers, reflecting the fact that a great deal of what we do in the working world consists of manipulating numbers, the problem with numbers is that when we get too many of them they become very difficult to work with. We cannot easily absorb a large set of numbers in our own minds and interpret them — especially if they aren't sorted into a nice order. We have either to reduce their quantity by means of statistics, or to represent them in terms of lines. Moreover, some aspects of working life are naturally graphical rather than numerical. The process of designing things always starts out by drawing, for example.

Thus the next natural step is to produce devices than can cope with lines, allowing both the user and the computer to draw pictures. The earlier picture devices were plotters and drafting machines, for output only, where the computer drew lines in ink on paper, or with a diamond on plastic. Later it became possible by means of the TV screen and an electronic 'light' pen for both computer and user to draw lines. We call such an arrangement a graphics scope.

Having, then, created devices for moving a pen in two dimensions, it does not require any extra technology to move it in three. We don't of course, have three-dimensional pieces of paper, but we do have three-dimensional hunks of metal, and we can replace the pen by a tool for cutting the metal. Thus it is an easy next step to make a computer-controlled milling machine. As a point of historical accuracy the computer-controlled milling machine preceded the drafting machine. However, this was a technological accident, and does not detract from the development of the philosophy of environmental devices.

Having established the fact that the computer can be made to register numbers and to move physical objects, we can combine these two facts and make it possible to create a *control* device of the computer. By this we mean observing the environment, comparing the observations with desired criteria and performing actions on the environment to bring it closer to those criteria.

Examples of computer control are the refining of oil, the

manufacture of paper and the post-operative monitoring of human beings. The range is gradually growing, but is limited not by the gadgets we can attach to the computer, but by our knowledge of the dynamics of the processes the computer is called upon to control. It is easy enough to construct devices for measuring temperature, pressure, liquid flow etc., and valves and switches that can be controlled by the computer. The problem is knowing precisely *what* to measure, and what the relationships should be between the measurements.

The last device we shall mention at this point is the ability of the computer to talk. That is, to couple the computer to a loudspeaker via a device which converts numbers to frequencies. Having recorded sentences spoken by human voice and converted them to strings of numbers, we can store these numbers in the computer and reconvert them to human voice on the way out again. Thus we can use the computer to produce stock answers to sets of stock questions.

Having described some, but by no means all, of the devices we can attach to the computer for the benefit of the people of the working world, I shall now attempt to create a means of classifying them. And one of the reasons for so doing is that such a classification provides a clue for the future development of the computer. It also gives you another blunt instrument to speak to your people with.

We now have enough devices to observe the existence of a two-dimensional array. In one dimension we have a spectrum of *transmission speeds* ranging from the very slow badge-reader to the high-speed graphics scope; in the other we have a spectrum of specialisation from the highly-coded ticket reservation terminal to the very general graphics scope. Let us call this the axis of *generality*.

Such a matrix is shown in Figure 6.1. Now you may argue about where each device lies, because I have not defined precisely what I mean by generality. And I don't propose to because for one thing there is no precise definition, and for another all I am attempting to do is to provide a little insight rather than some precise numbers. However, as an example of how this particular version was arrived at let me explain

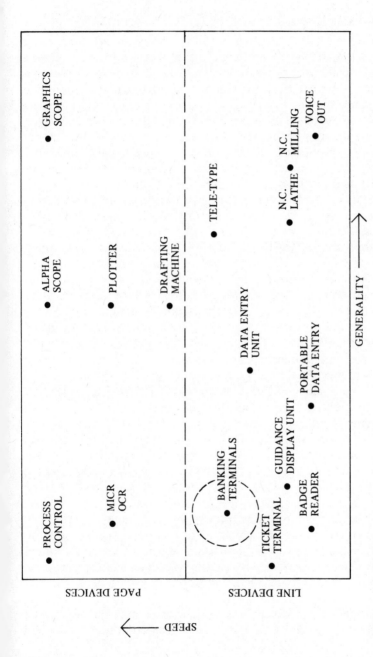

Figure 6.1 The put matrix

why I classify the Teletype as more general than the plotter. Although from the output point of view the plotter is more versatile, it can produce all the characters of the Teletype and as many more as you like, as well as draw continuous lines – which is really what it is for – against this is the superior power of the Teletype as an input device. Most plotters, indeed, have no input capability at all (however, some drafting machines can be used for *reading* drawings as well as producing them). Since we must regard input and output as equally necessary I have weighted Teletype input-output more heavily than continuous–line output. But this is only a personal whim which I don't want to detract from the general idea of the generality classification. The speed classification, on the other hand, is a more straightforward thing, and is really a function of data rate: how many numbers per second are transmitted during normal use.

We can, in turn, subdivide the speed category into low-speed and high-speed devices, which I have categorised as 'line' and 'page' devices in the figure, depending on whether the user is presented with a small amount of data at a time or a large amount.

The alphanumeric scope typically produces a *page* of output in response to a request. And typically the user makes note of some small part of the data displayed and uses that in his next step. He doesn't know quite what to expect, so he requests a wide range which he narrows after scanning the output. (Incidentally, scanning is a process in which the human being scores fairly well over the computer.) The user certainly doesn't copy the contents of the screen. When, occasionally, he does need the contents he can press a button which causes a separate printer to print it.

The drafting machine, plotter and graphics scope produce two dimensional drawings.   They are therefore *page processors,* without any discussion. Magnetic ink and optical character recognition are used for reading pages, but it some-times happens that a particular page, typically a bank cheque, consists only of a line or two.

Now although some of these devices may not always be directly connected *on-line,* they are all computer-controlled and therefore candidates for on-line usage. However, this is only a minor point. More important is the fact that most of them are neither input devices nor output devices, but both. Furthermore, in such cases we find the device oscillating frequently from one function to the other. In other words, the old-fashioned concept of an input stream and an output stream has given way to an oscillatory stream which we can call simply 'put'. And so I call the array of Figure 6.1 the 'put matrix'.

There are two reasons for arranging the user devices in this way. One is that it gives you a systematic way of talking about them with your people. And remember, they will have a strong tendency to involve you in the expense of the top right-hand corner, while you will want to drive them as closely as you can to the cheap, bottom left. And the other is that it provides us with a possible means for predicting the nature of future computer development. And it is a development in which more or less anyone can now take part. In the past, computer development has been the sole province of the manufacturer, and within the manufacturer's organisation has been essentially confined to the engineering department. But now that we can describe and discuss the computer in terms of user devices, there is nothing stopping any user from coming up with a bright idea.

The main emphasis in the future will be a very dense filling-out of the put matrix. In other words, now that engineers, managers, doctors etc. are beginning to discover what put devices mean they will bring forth ideas in abundance, and the manufacturers will respond by creating all kinds of special and general purpose equipment that will blend harmoniously into the application background. And applications will be bent more and more in the direction of the user.

Furthermore, we will no longer regard this equipment as 'peripheral' to the central computer. The adjective bears a connotation of after the fact or secondary, which, indeed, it has been. Put will become the *primary* consideration; competitions between the manufacturers will be won increasingly on the strength of it, and the details of the central computer will be a result of it. The elements of the put matrix are becoming the driving force of computer development, and you are all invited to the party.

No single person can be clever enough to predict what particular devices the future will herald. To know that is to know the details of many types of business. But if your business requires a device for telling the computer every time you open the door, it will be a cheap and simple matter to arrange. However, I am firmly convinced that there will be a very dense filling out of the bottom left-hand corner of the matrix. My reasons for believing this are that such devices are becoming easy to make and easy to connect to the computer, regardless of distance. It will be easy to produce 'families' of similar devices, possibly all looking alike to the computer, but appearing to be custom-built to the user. Many of them indeed will be portable. It will be an easy matter to obtain a close cooperation between potential user and designer, and it does not take a large company with large resources to produce them.

Two particularly powerful components of such devices are the micro-computer and the magnetic tape cassette. We now have fully-programmable computers that fit into a matchbox and weigh only a few grams. This enables us to catch a large proportion of the key-pressing errors at source without interrupting the central computer. And the cassette enables us to collect data in situations where it is physically difficult or uneconomical to be on-line. A typical combination of these two devices is the stocktaking terminal (portable data entry device). It hangs over the user's shoulder and weighs, in total, only a couple of kilos.

In short, the put matrix is the bow of the ship, and the direction is south-west. As to the costs of put devices, in the main these will come down substantially as the put matrix is filled out, as better methods of construction are invented and as costs are spread over substantially larger numbers. Specifically the prices of terminals that are in use today will almost inevitably remain the same. But when you consider that the put learning curve is some fifteen years behind the computer learning curve, you can readily predict substantial improvements in cost-performance. All the large manufacturers are attacking the put problem with vigour, and are being defiantly prodded by a large number of small manufacturers.

7 *But what will it cost you?*

Having held out the carrot of profitability and having tried to describe something of the nature of the computer we can now complete the balance sheet by looking into the question of what it all might cost you; or what it all ought to be costing, perhaps in contrast to what it is costing you right at this moment. Though even while this chapter is being written a hardware price war is in progress, the consequence of which will be profound and by no means short-lived.

Computing costs three times what the man said. And that doesn't include your time and the cost of the company lawyer. And then only if everything goes according to plan. If it doesn't, the only limit to the cost is the value of your company. It is easy to do things properly, but the opportunities for doing things improperly are frighteningly numerous. This chapter cannot hope to tell you to the penny what computing is costing you today, or will be costing you in the future. However there are certain guidelines to follow, and there are certainly a number of pitfalls to avoid.

Your main problem in discussing what computing ought to cost is that there is no descriptive language. It's not like buying a dozen eggs. As we said earlier, there are no absolute units of computing, and no one has ever made a broad survey of typical costs of typical applications in typical companies.

But having found ourselves some very thin ice, let us now go out and walk on it. At least we won't fall into hot water for trying.

The first thing you need is a blunt instrument for talking to your people with. Figure 7.1 is an example. It takes the form of a systematic family tree of types of computing which you should place on your desk every time you discuss new applications with anyone.

Before they start their first sentence get them to point to which branch of the tree they are going to talk about, and immediately you will have something of a clue as to the cost. Generally speaking, cost increases down the tree. But let us take a closer look.

Batch processing

The cheapest kind of computing is what we call batch processing. We bring a program and some data to the computer, stick it in the queue, run it when its turn comes, and take the output (if there is any) back to the user. There are flavours to this, however. Whether the program has a high priority and jumps to the head of the queue. Whether we use the post office, the company truck or the telephone system to carry the input and the output. But the going rate for this kind of computing is $20 per minute on a large, fast modern computer. All we cannot say is, what you can do with one minute of computer time — unless you are simply adding up numbers, in which case you can expect to be able to cope with some 60 million of them. But few of us have quantities of numbers of that magnitude.

Continuous processing

But the price of cheapness is paid for in delay. Most batch runs involve a cycle of twenty-four hours between pick-up of data and return of output. However an increasing amount of the world's work cannot tolerate such delays, and many applications cannot even tolerate delays of seconds. Hence the idea of the continuous mode, by which we mean that the

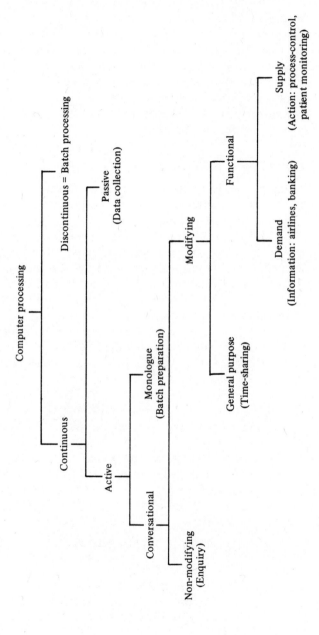

Figure 7.1 The types of computer processing (Reproduced from *The Corporate Computer* by the author)

program is live in the computer continuously, and is therefore usable whenever it is needed. This necessarily implies that
the user has at his disposal a gadget of some sort coupled to
the computer by means of telephone lines, as we discussed
in Chapter 6. This type of processing is normally called *real
time,* but very few applications do actually operate in the
time-frame of the environment, so the term is misleading.

Let us examine the flavours of continuous computing
starting at the bottom of the tree.

Functional processing

By functional processing I mean that the computer, or a
substantial part of it, is used for a single function, and that
either a large number of people use identical terminals in
conjunction with it, or it is attached to some equipment providing large amounts of data. Technologically, functional
computing comprises two modes: *demand* in which the user
demands information from the computer whenever he needs
it, e.g. ticket selling and inventory control, and *supply,* the
reverse of this, when the computer obtains information from
the environment when it needs it, e.g. process control and
patient monitoring. Furthermore, for cost estimating, purposes we can further see three basic subdivisions of this type
of computing.

The inventory problem: What have we got? As we said in
Chapter 4, in order to be really competitive many salesmen
today need to work from up-to-the-minute pictures of their
inventory. Examples are building materials, chemicals, drugs,
office supplies, travel tickets, hotel rooms, hospital beds, but
the list is much longer. And it is this point where we are going
to make one of the most important statements in this book.
In applications of this sort:

A COMPUTER IS AN ELECTRONIC BOOK

Instead of flipping the pages of a paper book containing
descriptions, quantities, prices and so on, we flip the pages
of an electronic book. The only difference, as far as the user
is concerned, is that what is written on the electronic pages

can be changed at will *at any time*. And the user need know
no more about the computer than the reader of a paper book
needs to know about printing presses. What could be simpler?

A computer is an electronic book.

To obtain a particular page takes typically a couple of
seconds, and flipping pages can take place at a speed to
deceive the eye. Moreover, all the users are presented with
exactly the same information at the same point in time.

A typical annual operating cost for such an inventory
application is $100,000, while the creation of a system
might cost some ten times this amount.

The vector problem: Where is it? The beds are in the hospital,
and the flanged plates are in the warehouse. But there are
other kinds of problem where objects are on the move, and
may be moving quite fast. And we need to keep very accurate
track of where they are moment by moment. For example
air traffic.

If air traffic is not too dense, a human operator can
monitor and control from a radar screen, but with all his
power of peripheral vision a human being cannot compete

with a high-speed computer when the density becomes too great. And with the vast speeds and distances of space travel there is no substitue for the computer. In these cases, for purposes of guaranteed safety, we need to know exact positions and speeds *this instant* so that corrective action can be taken. A jet aircraft moves 200 metres in a second, thus two planes on a collision course can be moving relatively at 400 metres per second. This means millisecond reaction at the very maximum. The cost is therefore much higher than in the inventory case. Aircraft move faster than their seats. But if the value of the project is that of a cloud of ten million dollar aircraft and the lives they carry, the cost is low at ten times the price of an inventory system.

There are problems which are hybrid with respect to these two classifications, for example that of railway trucks. The problem of locating trucks and predicting when they will be available is a tough one. In fact, during one of the frequent mail strikes in Italy a mountain of mail was moved out of Rome on railway trucks, and they were well into the following strike before they were found again.

Clearly railway trucks fall technically into the vector class, but because they move so slowly the economics of the system puts them in the inventory class.

The condition problem: What's going on? Since the discovery of bronze, man has been trying to exercise as tight a control as possible over the processing of materials in order to obtain a satisfactory yield. His problem has always been threefold, namely understanding the dynamics of the process, obtaining measurements of the variables, and then being able to do something about it. We find we can use the computer to help with the latter, the art of instrumentation engineering provides the means of measurement, and together they help the investigator analyse the process. Thus today we see a steadily growing application of the computer to the control of processes, involving complicated interactive systems of pressures, temperatures, flows of gases or liquids, compositions of mixes, etc. The key is knowing what is going on; to be able to ask questions of the condition of a large number of situations in the system, to compare these with desired conditions, and then to adjust valves, switches etc. to bring actual conditions in the direction of the desirable.

Although the condition problem found its genesis in industrial processes it has not been confined there. The human body is also an interactive system, indeed the most complicated one we know of. Under normal conditions it has an excellent control system, but occasionally it requires some form of external control. After a serious operation, for example open-heart surgery, it takes time for the body's own control mechanism to reassert itself, and one can help by sticking sensors in the patient and attaching these to a computer. The computer can then monitor the patient, turning on the blood tap and waking the nurse when necessary, thereby increasing the probability of his continued existence. Another example is the flow of traffic through a city. This may seem at first glance to be a vector problem, but because of the low speeds, physically determined routes, behaviour in packed queues, and continuous control by means of lights, it is technically a condition problem. Another is flight simulation in which we attach a cockpit mock-up to a computer programmed with the geometry of an aircraft and the dynamics of flight, in order to give a pilot a realistic impression of how the particular aircraft handles.

Most condition problems need millisecond reaction, but they also need a computer capable of very fast arithmetic because of the amount of interactive computation that has to take place within each time-frame. Such applications do not normally need much data storage, however, because they don't use data that is much more ancient than a few milliseconds. Consequently the cost of the computer itself can be very small, as low as $25,000 purchase price. But the cost of instrumentation can be high, and since each application is unique in detail, the cost of implementation can be high, typically ten times the hardware cost. But we cannot say more than this without going into particular detail.

I have mentioned costs as ranges and must stress that there is no general formula for predicting either the cost or the quality of the service. And not least of the reasons for this is that designing and implementing systems is an art, and artists are not equally gifted. If we measured service in terms of the numbers of 'transactions' per second of a particular kind, we might get two or twenty for the same price depending on the configuration and the quality of the implementation.

General purpose

In the functional mode the same program serves many users. In the general purpose mode each user has a different program. This means that the computer time is shared between them, hence the name 'time sharing'. Another fundamental difference between these two modes is that in the functional the user does not write the program. Indeed he need have no computing knowledge at all. Whereas in the general purpose mode the user very often writes his own programs, although he also has access to a library of programs written by others. In neither case is it necessary to know where the computer is located.

Symptomatic of time sharing is the individual who repeatedly wants to carry out a particular type of calculation. Thus a time sharing terminal gives the impression of being a very powerful desk calculator. The requirements of the task mean that the user needs immediate response, and since he is sharing time with many other users it is axiomatic that his program is short.

A terminal costs between $50 and $100 per month to rent, depending on type and rental agreement, plus some $10 per hour of actual use, including transmission. The cost of used computer time lies between $20 and $40 per minute. Note that this is higher than run-of-the-mill batch computing because the priority is much higher.

Enquiry

Everything we have discussed so far under the heading of continuous processing permits the user to *change* what is written on the electronic pages. Technologically this means that the contents of the files inside the computer can be changed at any time. This is a powerful weapon but it costs money. If you only want to look at the pages without being able to change them it costs about one third. So this becomes a very important question for you to ask. You must get your people to distinguish between 'on-line enquiry' and 'real-time update' as they are called in the trade. And if they propose the latter make them justify their claim.

To help you see the difference, selling from an accurate inventory necessarily needs real-time updating, otherwise the whole purpose is defeated. But suppose we decide to put the telephone catalogue in the computer so that the enquiry system uses an electronic book, there is little point in paying a premium for putting new subscribers in the system the instant their phone is installed. Suffice it to enter the new numbers and remove the old once every twenty-four hours, or even once a week. This so-called updating can be done very cheaply in batch mode.

Thus we see the existence of a class of applications in which we can enquire of the contents of a file, i.e. read an electronic page, but cannot change it, i.e. we cannot *write* on the pages. Hence the classification 'enquiry' or 'non-modifying' mode. And the importance of the distinction is that enquiry mode systems are much easier and cheaper to create, and are about one third the cost of modifying systems to run.

Conversational versus monologue

Everything we have talked about so far under the heading Continuous consists of some sort of 'dialogue' or 'conversation' between the user and the computer. The user 'speaks' a sentence, i.e. he enters some characters on a keyboard, and the computer 'replies' with a line or page of characters, on basis of which the user enters another sentence, and so on. We call this the 'conversational' mode. But it is also possible to have a one-way conversation in which the user inserts characters but receives no reply from the computer other than the message was received. We can call this the 'monologue' mode. And, as you might expect, this is much cheaper than the conversational.

Typical of the monologue mode is remote batch preparation. Here we use the continuous mode to initiate the dis-
continuous, i.e. to place a program and set of data in the
batch queue. This is achieved by means of a terminal compri-
sing a keyboard and possibly a card-reader or tape unit. The
program itself may be permanently catalogued in the computer, while the data may be transmitted from the terminal.
The object of the exercise is to enter a program as soon as
the data is ready without suffering the delay of the company
mail or whatever.

Active versus passive

All the varieties of processing described above require the
computer to do something, even though the immediate
output may not amount to much. Hence the description, the
active mode. However we may wish to send data to the computer as it occurs, but not have the computer actually act on
it at the time of transmittal. Thus the computer plays a
passive role, and a typical example is that of data-acquisition.
Here we might have a number of simple devices scattered
about the factory, the lab or wherever, in which the users
insert simple cards or plastic badges, or twiddle knobs and
push buttons. Typical applications are registering arrival
and departure times of people, parts or tools at a particular
work station. Thus these devices provide the fundamental
data about the work in hand: hours worked, where, on what
job, where everything is, what has been completed and what
hasn't.

The devices themselves are usually very simple and cheap:
as low as $30 a month. The computer time involved is almost
negligible, and the systems are easy to create, because we
aren't calling upon the computer to do very much. Therefore
the monologue mode is extremely cheap and, because it is
simple, is extremely reliable. Probably the main expense is
the processing of the day's data in the batch mode at night.
But this, again, is cheaper than the continuous mode, trans-
for transaction.

This completes the picture. Precise numbers depend upon

precise applications, but this classification provides the basis for a comparative picture and a means of getting your people to explain themselves to you.

Having looked at costs in a systematic way we can now discuss the elements that make up these costs. But in doing so I should issue a clear warning that prices vary in all directions, from year to year, from manufacturer to manufacturer, from country to country. Moreover what a computer consists of in detail varies from make to make, and there is no industry standard terminology for many of the devices. When you get into detail it is extremely difficult to say what you mean, and any general discussion about costs has to be hedged about with disclaimers. Nevertheless we ought to be able to get the orders of magnitude right.

Enlarging on what we said about the evolution of complexity in Chapter 5, in the early years a computer was a computer, whereas today a computer is an assemblage of items selected from a very long list of possibilities. In the early years the name or the number of a computer was sufficient to characterise it completely, whereas today it characterises only the central processing unit, a steadily diminishing item as regards both physical size and price. Today a full description of the hardware configuration of a computer can comprise several sheets of paper, whereas before it consisted of a single sentence.

Bearing this in mind the hardware cost of today's computer is the sum of a large number of contributory costs, of which the c.p.u. can be quite minor. This is particularly true of the smaller machines.

An associated problem is that of being sure that you have remembered to include all the items, and haven't left out some vital module whose absence will render the entire ensemble inoperative. There seems to be no guaranteed method of doing this, and one can only advocate repeated, painstaking analysis of the design and reading of the fine print.

Even the smallest IBM computer contains a list of well over a hundred hardware items to be selected in designing the configuration. Naturally, your technical people will be responsible for doing this, but it is important that you realise that they have a problem.

And you should be warned that as the details come out your initial enthusiasm will wane. It is now possible to buy a computer for as little as $10,000, but it will cost you $100,000!

Ranges of prices

Central processing units (c.p.u.'s)

By c.p.u. we mean some memory, an arithmetic unit, and an operator's console including some kind of typewriter. The memory can vary in size and the arithmetic unit in speed. The minimum memory size of a computer of any appreciable applicability is 8K words or 16K bytes, where a word may consist of between 16 and 72 bits, and a byte of 8 bits. On the other hand a typical large memory may consist of 256K words of a million bytes, and can even be larger. Memory and arithmetic unit cycle times can vary from a few microseconds down to a tenth of a microsecond or so, and it is this factor alone that is characterised by the name of the computer.

The range of c.p.u. prices is very large indeed, varying from $10,000 for a 16K byte memory of several microseconds cycle time, to almost $5 million for a 4 million byte memory of half a microsecond; i.e. roughly $1 per byte.

Machine room input–output (I/O)

Most computers require some sort of card-reader and high-speed printer in the machine room. There is very little that one can do with a c.p.u. unattached to the means of getting data into and out of it. And even at this point any initial hope we may have had of a cheap computer begins to fade because a single printer costs more than the cheapest c.p.u.

Printers capable of from 300 to 1200 lines per minute cost between $10,000 and $30,000, while card readers of similar speeds cost between $6,000 and $10,000.

But between any piece of equipment and the c.p.u. we need channels, and these come in two basic types, high-speed (selector) and low-speed (multiplex), for secondary storage and I/O respectively. Typical prices of these channels lie between $1000 and $10,000.

The number of channels you order will depend upon how many of the devices that use them you want to run simultaneously.

Secondary storage

A c.p.u. in isolation is not a data handler. It may have sufficient capacity to carry out arithmetic that doesn't require much data, and may be sufficient to act as a control device to an industrial process, but it is not capable of carrying out functions typical of the modern commercial company of any appreciable size. To perform data-handling we need some form of large scale, secondary storage. Traditionally this has been magnetic tape, but this is supplemented today by magnetic disc or drum, which in turn will be giving way to very large scale stationary memory devices as the technology and economics permit.

Prices vary with size, speed, reliability, ease of operation, age and manufacturer. The price of a standard 2400 foot reel tape unit varies between $10,000 and $50,000. A fairly good rule of thumb for disc is a price of 5000 bytes per dollar, and for drum 100 bytes per dollar. And don't forget the channels!

Terminals

The computer is being used more and more in the continuous mode as the economics improve and as the need becomes justified. That is to say, there is an increasing use of remote terminals of one kind and another, attached to the computer over telephone lines, as described in Chapter 6. But we shall limit ourselves here to three types in order to give an impression of the cost scale. The first of them is the hard-copy, character-by-character typewriter or teletype, of which a typical price range is $1000 to $4000. If this type of device is too slow for the application we can go to the alphanumeric scope whose price range is about the same, depending on size and complexity. If alphanumerical characters are insufficient, and the application requires the ability to depict drawings, we must move to the graphic scope whose price range varies between $4000 and $40,000, again depending on size and versatility.

Again, don't forget the channels!

Transmission

To attach computing equipment to telephone lines requires equipment at both ends of the line to convert digital numbers into appropriate carrier frequencies and back again. These devices are called modems (modulator-demodulators) and cost between $1000 and $5000 depending on speed. In addition to this is the cost of the lines.

Other vital equipment

The preceding paragraphs deal only with the obvious equipment, the stuff that appears in the diagrams. In addition there is a lot of treacherous territory that is frequently overlooked until the fatal day arrives when the whole caboodle is switched on. This is the equipment that ties the major items together into a functioning unit, such equipment as adaptors, synchronisers, buffers, controllers and indicators. The total cost of this kind of equipment may not be so great, and the important thing is to make sure that it isn't forgotten. However the cost of missing items might have affected the result of a competition, and this may not be discovered until long after the award has been won.

It would be very tempting to follow this up by a few lists of detailed configurations, but this would scare you off for ever. Instead we'll content ourselves with the totals for two or three different levels to give you a rough idea.

Beginning at the traditional low end there is a lot of talk about mini-computers these days as though they were a new idea. In fact they are a very old idea. There have been mini-computers since the 1950s. Moreover a mini only remains a mini as long as we don't build it up with secondary storage, terminals and so forth, which is what often happens.

A typical mini c.p.u. costs $10,000, but when the c.p.u. has been decorated with channels and devices the price can easily be $100,000.

At the medium level the c.p.u. will cost in the neighbourhood of half a million dollars, whereas the total cost might be about a full million. At the top level the c.p.u. may be up to about $2 million, of a total price of perhaps $3 million.

Outside this spectrum lie microcomputers, about the size of a matchbox, and very large computers used by defence agencies and atomic energy people. The latter are outside the scope of the normal business organisation, whereas the former are evolving so rapidly that all you can say is that they are very cheap indeed, and you wonder whether perhaps the bottom isn't dropping out of the hardware market.

These are the kinds of price you have to pay if you buy your own equipment, or the equivalent if you rent. However if you use a computer service bureau you must somehow compare their prices with what you would have paid, and try to compute a trade-off. But this isn't easy, not least because you are comparing the prices of raw hardware against those of a service.

I started the chapter by saying that computing costs three times what the man said, and by that I mean that, as a rule of thumb, the cost of creating programs is about the same as that of the hardware, and the cost of operating may not be much less. In time, however, the figure will be greater than three because people costs will continue to rise, while hardware costs will fall.

Creating a system

Having set the stage, this next section deals with the problems of carrying out management's intentions and getting computer systems working. There are some solutions, but they are outweighed by the problems. If there were cut and dried solutions to everything you wouldn't be necessary. But you are, and your unique managerial style will ensure a set of solutions that will differ from anyone else's. The important thing is to know what the problems are likely to be — and well in advance. This section also continues the discussion about costs and benefits — with the same reservations as in Section 1.

8 Using the computer

In the beginning there was never any discussion with management about how to use a computer. Computers never came about as a solution to a distinct problem stated by a manager of any organisation. On the other hand they didn't just happen. There has always been a deep desire in the human breast to perform arithmetic automatically, accurately and hopefully fast. And this has been no low-level aspiration or occupation undertaken by second class minds. The invention of the place-value system, so natural to the five-year old once he understands it, was a stroke of genius, although we don't know the inventor's name. The Romans never had it although goodness knows they desperately needed it, with the numbers of people and the vast economy that they were trying to manage. Try multiplying XXXIV by CCXVII! And the place-value system enabled some other genius to invent the abacus. Later on we had such mathematician-philosophers as Pascal and Leibnitz inventing desk calculators, and in the nineteenth century Charles Babbage who laid down the specifications for the computer a hundred years before his time.

Perhaps the whole thing is summed up in Babbage's cry of frustration when he found a lot of errors in some tables that were being computed (by hand of course) for the Astronomer Royal. 'I wish to God these calculations had been executed by steam.' We shall come back to Charles Babbage in a moment because he did a lot more than try to build computers out of brass. Suffice it to say that this deep human urge to do automatic arithmetic found its expression among mathematicians and not among businessmen or managers, even though today the latter are the overwhelming users of the outcome.

The computer was rightly invented as the solution to a problem. But once it began to work and to be produced in serious quantities the solution began to chase the problems. In the early days you could be forgiven for supposing that the computer was invented for no reason at all other than as an amusing electronic toy. But the same was true of aircraft, for example. They weren't invented to satisfy the needs of the airlines. At first their main use was aerobatics, a source of amusement to their builders, and later to the general public. Only after a period of years did the solution create the problem, that of high speed, long distance travel, and the carrying of the mails.

In the case of the computer, the original nature of the arithmetic was very limited. It consisted of producing mathematical tables with more accuracy and precision than had been possible before: the arithmetic of science. However it took time before the idea of applying it to the arithmetic of business caught on. It is true that punched card machinery had been around for fifty years, but because it did not contain a stored program it was severely limited in application, and was more or less restricted to doing the book-keeping. But organisations contain a great deal of hidden arithmetic, a fact not widely realised in 1950, and after two decades of catalysis from the computer this arithmetic has burst forth out of hiding and has become a part of modern life.

We have dignified the concept of business arithmetic with the name *information,* and in Appendix 1 we shall discuss the nature of information in some detail. For the purposes of this chapter the most important thing to say about information is that there is an infinite amount of it, so given a computer of arbitrary size you can always find a problem that will be too big for it to handle. As computers have got bigger, problems have got bigger, and this has led to even bigger computers and hence to the guarantee of the eternal perpetuation of the computer industry.

Information is infinite, but it's not all equally useful or

accurate. That the moon is made of green cheese is false and useless. The pedigree of the bull chasing you across the field though true, is also useless. However, the noise of its galloping hoofs is true and most useful, in that it causes adrenalin to be secreted into your blood stream, which speeds you up. The statement that your secretary liked your new tie was false but useful in that it brightened up an otherwise deadly dull day. Your problem as a manager is to determine what, of all the infinite amount of information that you could get hold of, would do you the most good.

In the final analysis you and only you can decide what's best for you — at any level and in any occupation. But you can get help. There is a large army of people today who work in the professions of Operational Research and Systems Analysis, and their task in life is to look at organisations to find out how they operate and how they could be made to operate better. Their ranks have grown along with the computer, as a direct result of it, and by now a great deal of knowledge has been built up about other organisations which might be able to help you locate the sources of profit in yours that we talked about in Chapter 4.

Probably the first bit of operational research that was ever undertaken was Charles Babbage's discovery that the cost of sending a letter was independent of the distance, and was almost entirely the cost of the organisations at each end. However, great credit must also be assigned to Sir Rowland Hill who actually believed what Babbage told him, and who therefore inaugurated the penny post. To most people it was patently untrue. It stood to reason that the further the letter travelled the more horses and man hours it took. And so it is today. A lot of things are obviously true until you actually extract the arithmetic from them. A good example comes from war-time Britain. Instructions were sent out from the Ministry of Fuel that in order to win the war Britons should never wash under running water, never take a shower, and use only five inches of water in the tub. I immediately put the plug in the bath, and found that after an enjoyable, relaxing and cleansing shower I had accumulated only one inch of water. In other words, to speed the day of victory the rules

should have been reversed and showers issued to all house-
holds. Whitehall never even acknowledged my letter. It isn't
always easy to convince people. And that probably goes for
you too.

And another problem is that, like information itself, not
all purveyors of information are equally useful. Operational
Research started during the war, and not a single OR worker
had a degree in the subject. They were physicists, chemists,
economists, indeed anyone with the right attitude and a stop
watch. They did some impressive work and saved thousands
of lives. But in the 1950s OR became a university subject,
often in the Department of Mathematics, and publications
became more and more learned, and less and less useful. It's
not that today's OR worker means any harm. It's just that
the integral sign at the end of this paper isn't much help to
the manager who is presumably supposed to implement the
idea. Examination answers and doctoral theses are evaluated
by other OR people and not by the consumers of the product. So you may experience difficulty in finding someone
genuinely interested in helping you, rather than someone
who finds your problem a fascinating source of publishable
solutions.

There's no formula for success in finding good people. It's
more or less useless looking at academic qualifications. Really
the only way to find a good man is to go by reputation.
Take your cap in hand and ask your competition who helped
them. Good people do exist, but there aren't many of them
so they're rather busy, and you may have to wait.

But supposing you are lucky, how do you set about getting
things on to the computer?

The firing order

Step one is to locate the sources of profit and to arrange
them in a single series according to some criteria. The
criteria could be in order of:

Decreasing apparent profitability

Increasing apparent difficulty

Increasing guessed elapsed time to complete

Function within the organisation

Decreasing credibility

Decreasing probability of success

or some criteria of your own. But whatever you choose, let it be a *single* series. Let us call it the firing order. We shall say more about the firing order in Chapter 10

Techniques

The essential link between locating sources of potential profit and putting the computer to work to realise them is to be able to conjure up the necessary techniques that the computer is to be called upon to carry out. Such techniques exist at a wide range of levels of sophistication, many of them well-known from former times. The finance systems require the standard techniques of cost-accounting, discounted cash flow etc., while bridge design may require use of the finite element method. As we move away from the working level, however, it may not be at all obvious what techniques to use, and a lot of work may have to be done to find out in each particular case. We are no longer simply slopping old techniques on to new equipment, but applying brand new techniques to our way of life that we've never used before. And many of these techniques fall into the category dignified by the appendage, management science, which is discussed in the next chapter.

Determining appropriate techniques does not really constitute a step in itself, but is inextricably implicit in the steps that follow.

Systems requirements and design

The next step is to undergo a detailed analysis of the first
system (or first three systems) in the firing order. This
analysis takes time and contributes to the cost side of the
economic picture. Don't make the mistake of neglecting
the necessary budget at this stage. The analysis consists of
collecting detailed information about the procedures as they
are today, and ideas about what they should be in the future.
Together these constitute the requirements of the new
system. But they cannot be produced *in vaccuo*. They must
always make sense within a framework of technological possibility. Therefore the requirements and the design evolve
out of an iterative dialogue between the using department
and the computing department, the latter holding a subordinate dialogue with the manufacturers.

It must be emphasised here that this detailed analysis will
produce a much more accurate profit picture as wild guesses
are replaced by reasonable estimates. And it can happen that
the new economic picture can change the firing order, and
even eliminate an entire system, or delay its implementation
for some years in the hope that new technology will make a
substantial improvement. Furthermore, the economic picture
will change twice more, as the estimates for implementation
and operation become actual expenses, and as the estimates
of value become reality (to the extent that they are amenable
to objective measurement). The systems will be implemented
in phases of increasing scope. The details are described in
Chapter 11, and the problems of managing them in Chapter 12.

Software

Having evolved a system design, the implementation team
then sets to work in an environment of software. *To the user
the computer equals its software.* Software provides the
capability and strongly influences the throughput of the
computer.

It is important, then, that you are satisfied that your

people are using the right software and that the software works.

The role of the user starts at the point either of writing the programs that he shall use, or of obtaining them from some third party or from the manufacturer along with the computer. But whether you write your own programs or commission someone else to write them, the end result is that someone, somewhere has the task of getting the computer to work productively. The important point to understand is that to the programmer the computer consists of its software. And to a great extent, the same is true of the operator. It is true that the operator physically handles the hardware, he puts the cards in the card reader, mounts and dismounts tapes, tears paper off the printer. But he also presses buttons on the console, types in messages to the operating system and receives messages back from the operating system. All button-pushing and message sending is done via the software.

So, in a very real sense the computer is the software and not the hardware. But is is rather difficult to get management to realise this. Software is intangible to all save the programmer. You don't see it coming through the door on a fork-lift truck. You can't invite your friends from the golf club to come and see your compilers.

But it is the software that will let you down much more than the hardware. And, unless you lay down strict managerial rules, the software will keep changing. It doesn't change of its own accord, but the manufacturers keep 'improving' it with engineering changes called *new releases*. You are not forced to adopt every new release that comes along, but your technical people will always have a good story for doing so. New releases are always well-intended but *someone always suffers*. Some good old reliable program that used to run every night suddenly won't run any more, but the hardware hasn't been touched. (This in itself ought to be proof that the computer consists of its software!) The problem is that the software, like every other computer program, will contain errors when it first hits the field. There is a limit to the amount of testing the manufacturer can do in his arti-

But it is the software that will let you down much more than the hardware.

ficial environment. The real test of any program is daily running, a guarantee that *things will go wrong at first.*

The managerial solution is plenty of spare-time dummy-running with your own production programs until you have found all the errors you can, and a limit to the frequency of installing new versions of the software. Try to keep it down to once a year.

A consequence of the fact that the computer equals its software is that in choosing the computer configuration you must ensure that the software is appropriate. If you want to run in so-called real-time, a batch operating system won't do you much good. But there is more to it than that. Both a batch and a real-time operating system come in many flavours.

There is a lot of detail that must be gone into, and you will want to see some sort of proof from your technical people that they have asked all the questions and got all the right answers. Computer capability depends on the software, which in turn is partly dependent on the hardware.

But so is throughput, and the two *compete*. The more complicated the software the higher the overhead and the less the productive work it can carry out. It is vital to realise this. You cannot have your softcake and eat it. Have a clear statement of the need for each new version. If it is 'increased throughput' all well and good, but if it is 'improved capability' beware that it will be at the cost of something, and be quite clear what that something is before allowing the installation of the new version.

Hardware

The function of hardware is *to carry the software*. Once your requirements are expressed in terms of software it should be a fairly straightforward matter to determine con-figurations of hardware that will enable the software to operate.

The main differences between various choices of hardware will be the speeds with which the software elements work, and the amounts of memory that the software requires. Some hardware is created with a proper understanding of the requirements of software, while other hardware is not. And the difference in cost and speed can be enormous.

The hardware description will consist of a picture backed up by several pages of item numbers. Don't attempt to read or understand this description. Content yourself that your technical people understand the necessity for it all, in terms of the software, and have a statement in the contract binding the manufacturer to supply, free of charge, any omitted items.

Hardware maintenance and reliability

Although computers these days are very solid state and

deeply integrated, they still contain a lot of moving mechanical parts that are subject to fair wear and tear. Even today's electronic components are not free of possible malfunction. Computers therefore need regular hardware maintenance.

From the cost point of view, all rental contracts provide for maintenance, but separate maintenance contracts have to be entered into in the case of purchase. The price of a maintenance contract depends, of course, upon the amount of equipment, how difficult it is to diagnose and repair, and so on. But as a rule of thumb it is three to five per cent of the purchase price.

Then comes the question of scheduling preventative maintenance. The manufacturer needs to run diagnostics on each item of equipment with a certain frequency, but is usually fairly flexible about when this can occur. Your interest is to meet his requirements, but at a time of the day or week that is least inconvenient to you. And you should always schedule your work so that he has more time than he thinks he needs, because once the maintenance engineers start to tinker there is absolutely no guarantee that they will get it started again. All too frequently the machine is down because the engineers took it for preventive maintenance.

Emergency maintenance can occur at any time. Whenever the operators suspect something wrong this is reported immediately to the maintenance engineers. Diagnosing the error and repairing the equipment can take minutes or weeks, and it can affect the entire computer or only an individual unit. Depending on the seriousness of the case and the queue of unprocessed work, you have to start considering back-up arrangements. If you have only one computer you will want a standing agreement with the owner of a similar configuration for mutual back-up such as that after a certain amount of elapsed time from a breakdown the back-up installation is warned, work is prepared for transmittal etc., so that by a certain deadline production can begin on the back-up machine.

You will want to see the details of the back-up arrangement, and will probably want to have one or two emergency fire drills to see that it actually works. It won't. And this will give you a golden opportunity of showing the computing department who's boss.

As a regular by-product of maintenance you should require incident reports, signed by the engineers and the operators, which can be used at regular performance meetings. We shall return to this in Chapter 22.

Engineering changes

Like the software, the hardware doesn't sit still. The manufacturer's engineering department is constantly improving the hardware, resulting in physical changes which have to be installed by the field engineers at nights and on weekends. Again, like the software, these can lead to unintended problems and down-time, sometimes extending to days.

Unless you insist on it the manufacturer won't bother you with the details of hardware changes, and will install them whenever he gets the change. This can be a constant source of shock, and you will probably want to know what is going on.

Engineering changes come in four flavours:

i) Reliability. They are currently using a defective device which is causing a malfunction, and are replacing it with something much more reliable.

ii) Capability. They have found a way of slightly speeding up the arithmetic unit, improving the precision of multiplication, attaching more tape units to a channel, or some other improvement to the capability of the hardware.

iii) Error-correction. Errors have been discovered in the design or the manufacture that are causing intermittent failure, and a redesigned or refabricated part is to be substituted.

iv) Serviceability. It is difficult to foresee what problems a new computer is going to encounter during servicing, and it is often necessary to do some redesign after delivery to make servicing easier, quicker and more reliable.

Of these, capability is the least interesting. You obtained a computer that was capable of doing the job and you are presumably content with this for a time, after which you may make a substantial jump to something new. The other three types of engineering change are vital, however, because they all generate reliability. Serviceability means more diagnostics during preventative maintenance periods and less time needed to locate and repair faults, hence a more reliable machine.

You should be aware of the size of the backlog of un-installed changes, which of these are really vital and which are only advisable, how long each will take to do and what back-up will be provided if the machine does not recover in time. And you should be the one who specifies when the installation shall take place. If you manage the engineering change activity you will minimise the possible resulting down time.

Application programs

By far the biggest problem is that of the application pro-grams. The software and the hardware are produced by com-panies who do nothing else but this. They install the same in hundreds of places, and they know it intimately. They are professional at their job, and there is every reason to expect that the machinery will function. Writing programs is a little different. In all probability the programs you use will be written by your own employees and will not be used by anyone else. Although your systems designers and program-mers may be professionals they may not have much experi-ence, and your programs won't get the exhaustive testing that a large group of users could give them. The using

departments may not be too clever at stating their requirements, or may not even be too clear about what they want.
The criteria for the quality of the programs may not be explicitly stated. Not enough machine time may be allocated
to check-out. There are all sorts of reasons why programming
goes wrong.

The upshot is that programs always take longer to write,
cost more, run less efficiently, etc., than was expected or
promised. But this problem is complicated, and we shall
return to it from time to time in various contexts.

Operations

The actual running of the computer must be as rugged and
business-like as you can make it. Here is part of your organisation's life-blood. Once the application programs have been
accepted by the using department, vital company procedures
are committed to the computer for guaranteed running by
guaranteed times, producing guaranteed results. This is the
biggest commitment that the computing department has. It
may not hurt the organisation if a new program is delayed in
implementation, but it will certainly hurt if the implemented
program is delayed in running. If the factory doesn't receive
its instructions, work stops. If the pay cheques are late you
may have a strike on your hands. If the material orders aren't
out in good time you may have a shortage in the warehouse.

Operations must be a tight organisation, well trained and
drilled, with competent staff and leadership. Your criteria of
success should be that you never hear complaints about
dropped decks of cards, delayed or even lost output,
destroyed magnetic tapes, unverified punching and so on.

The costs of operations vary as much as the costs of the
computer, from a three-man, one-shift team, with everyone
trained on everything, to a ten-man, three-shift regiment
with squads of people responsible for particular aspects of
the operation, tape library, console, card-reader and printer,
and so on. Operations will probably include key-punching,

which can be anything from one girl, part-time, to a room full of operators.

Training

One of the standard omissions in installing new systems is that of training the potential users. Time and time again it happens, even amongst the most sophisticated of computer users. Training is the Cinderella of systems and you'd better take the glass slipper in your own hand. You must decide right at the outset who is going to be responsible for the training, who needs to be trained and in what, what information is going to be needed, who is supposed to provide it and when. The trouble with training is that, unless your company has a training department, there is no one who has the obvious responsibility. Even if one does have such a department, computing may lie beyond its traditional ken. So you may have to force a gunshot marriage of computing with training.

The constant argument that you will get from the programmers as the training people try to force the necessary information out of them is that they aren't quite ready. If they reveal their hand today they may have to change it tomorrow. And anyway they can't take precious time away from doing the job.

Achieving a balance between too much training and too little, too early and too late, between training man and programmer will call upon the Houdini in you like nothing else within this field.

9 Management science

Management, whatever it is, certainly isn't a science, so why put everyone off by having a chapter with a phoney name? Well, the trouble is that the term has entered the language and indeed our culture. There are university departments with Management Science in the title. The fact is that what management science is all about is all very valid. It's the title that's wrong. The title ought to be something like, Arithmetical Crutches in Decision-Making, or Managerial Information Amplifiers, or Numerical Energy for Jaded Executives. But is isn't, and there's not much hope of changing it, so instead let's try to explain it.

Really it ought not to need explaining because so much has already been published on the subject. But the accent has been on the science and not on the management. Very little has been written that the run of the mill manager can have a hope of understanding, even though in the last resort if he doesn't use the techniques that this subject embraces there's not much point in having the subject.

Having established our credentials, why should we be interested in management science in the context of this book? It is because a reasonable understanding of the techniques involved will help you in isolating the sources of profit. It will help you discuss them with the OR people and the systems analysts. And they aren't difficult. I find them much easier to understand than double-entry book-keeping.

To start out let us remind ourselves what science is. This ought to be a healthy exercise because so much nowadays is reckoned to be scientific — as well as democratic and non-polluting. We all know what we mean by the scientific approach when applied to the laboratory. We construct apparatus for measuring something, and we use it for observing the effect of one variable on another, holding everything else constant; the behaviour of the volume of gas as a result of changes in pressure, holding the temperature constant, for instance.

We analyse the observations and make learned postulates about them. From the postulates we make predictions of new situations, we make new measurements and compare them with the predictions, find they don't quite agree, adjust our new postulates and recycle. Here we have in mind such sciences as physics and chemistry, and the essence of this kind of science is our ability to exercise complete control over the experiment. I don't suppose there's any doubt in most people's minds that this process is a part of science.

You can't always, however, exercise complete or even partial control over the other variables, and you are then prevented from observing directly the effect of one upon the other. In that case the effects of the variables in which you are not interested have to be removed by means of the technique known as statistics. For example agriculture and physiology. You can't fix the temperature, so you can't measure the direct effect of rainfall on growth. But you can come close enough for all practical purposes by taking measurements over a sufficiently long period of time, providing enough statistics to remove the effect of temperature. And this is still science. And so far everything we do is objective. The only differences in our results stem from our varying ability to read the instruments.

But there are other kinds of science in which subjective judgements come into play, for example psychology and sociology. You can argue whether these are sciences or not, but for our present purposes let us suppose they are. What is of interest to us is where management lies in this spectrum, if at all. The answer is that it is both everywhere and nowhere. Management entails so many different things that we can find scientific techniques that are usable from the fully determined, the statistical and the subjective classes, and we can find manifestations of management that do not seem to be amenable to any kind of science at all. If the last weren't true we would find the upper levels of our organisation staffed with scientists. Most aspects of management are a very personal matter, entirely unamenable to scientific methods. And this is just as true of the manager today as it was of Atilla the Hun and Genghis Khan. J.B. Farrington-Gurney has the advantage over them of the telephone, Xerox, Scotch tape and the capacity for doing high-speed arithmetic. But these things haven't *replaced* him.

Even if the major premise of management is one of human nature and individual character, a single individual operates at many different levels simultaneously, and at some of the lower levels there are aspects that lend themselves to the scientific approach and the use of the computer, freeing time and energy for the less tractable problems. What really happens then is that these aspects get delegated to a system of some sort, and no longer belong to the realm of management. Or looking at it the other way, management comes in when all else fails.

Broadly speaking we can group scientific methods into two classes, profit squeezing and profit seeking. By profit squeezing I mean changing current ways of doing things to reduce wastage, inefficiency, queues etc., thereby creating more profit out of existing goods and services; while by profit seeking I mean determining new products, processes or services, locating new plant, invading new territory etc. to create new sources of profit.

Profit squeezing

By profit squeezing, then, we mean creating new procedures within the existing organisation and with regard to the existing products in order to reduce the wastage of time, materials and money. In most organisations procedures evolve slowly with time, and very rarely does anyone step back to take a critical look at the way things are done. There are several reasons for this. In the first place someone has to realise that something might be wrong. Then there's the question of who is going to do it? Everyone is so busy. How do you do it? No one in the organisation has any experience in these things. Can we really expect any improvements? Everyone knows their job so well. They've been doing it for years and they are such a faithful bunch of employees. It would be difficult to expect much return on the investment. On the other hand, time-honoured tradition is no guarantee at all of efficiency. On the contrary, it can be an excellent guarantee of tenure in jobs that ought not to exist. Most companies have a Keeper of the King's Keys in their employ. You will always meet a lot of counter-arguments that you will have to combat in your own sweet way. But the chances are good that they will be well worth combating.

Let us start by looking in some detail at a typical example, that of using the computer to allocate resources and schedule activities. Examples of scheduling problems: shipping, city transport, delivery to customers, manufacturing, the piping of oil, school timetables. They are characterised by the chronological ordering of events involving people, places, equipment and action. In addition, since there must be some purpose to the order, it must be such as to best satisfy a set of criteria of some sort.

This is a necessarily vague definition. What kinds of people? What kinds of action? What kinds of criteria? What do you mean by best? How do you decide? What methods do you use for producing the schedule? Why do you need a computer all of a sudden? These are the questions that will put the meat of the discussion on the bones of the definition. There are a lot of answers, but at the same time there is a commonality which makes the study of scheduling as a single subject a worthwhile endeavour.

An additional thought is the answer to the question, what is non-scheduling? Non-scheduling is allowing events to happen at random with no thought for the social or economic consequences. Much of life is run in a non-scheduled manner, and rightly so, but there do exist activities in which events occur at random where a good case could be put for introducing a schedule.

The locked-up profit in scheduling problems can be due to one or more of the following:

Unemployed people or machinery due to late arrival of materials.

Overconsumption of time and fuel in unoptimum routes.

Unused rooms or equipment.

An excess of storage facilities due to irregular deliveries.

Time spent in queues.

Too many employees in the scheduling department itself.

The basic problem with scheduling is that there are usually so many possible combinations of events, thousands or even millions, that unaided human beings simply cannot explore them all, or even a worth-while fraction of them. So there is little hope of achieving an optimum, and consequently there is a guarantee of wastage.

I have not attempted any classification of scheduling situations, although a useful purpose might be served in so doing. One can however see examples of scheduling that takes place occasionally (buses and schools), frequently (oil, shipping, manufacturing) and continuously (computer work-load). One can also see other differences. For example, in a school timetable, if Mr Brown is due to take 5C for French the first period Thursday morning it is assumed that Mr Brown can teach French, at least to the standard required by 5C. In a factory schedule, on the other hand, it may not be possible to assume that the details of the job are known to the employees. The schedule itself can contain the operating instructions. In other words the schedule might embrace each basic operation, drilling, rivetting, planing, etc.

In obtaining solutions to these problems our first task is always to state clearly the criteria that we wish to satisfy by means of our schedule. This may sound a rather trite statement, but one often encounters situations where the goals are not stated explicitly and there exists no way of judging the quality of the final product. Top management of companies are not always innocent of not stating the goals of their enterprises, (see *Up the Organisation* by Peter Townsend).

Following the criteria we must next state the constraints that a solution must satisfy. Only then can we begin to determine what algorithms, i.e. mathematical methods, would be most appropriate for the solution. At this stage we can say that

criteria + constraints + algorithms = 'program'

whether the program is a computer program or simply a series of tasks to be performed by hand. Without the computer however these ideas are usually only academic exercises because of the speed factor.

Let us consider some examples of each factor.

Criteria What are the goals that the schedule should satisfy?

Maximum profit for the company?

Minimum cost of operating the service?

Best possible quality of service within a stated budget?

Simplest working rhythm?

Maximum deployment of facilities?

Most satisfactory human circumstances?

Minimum wear and tear, hence maintenance costs?

Usually we encounter a hierarchy of criteria to be satisfied in order of importance until there are no options left to us.

Constraints What are the limitations that the schedule must satisfy?

Physical: One batch of oil cannot pass another in the pipeline.
              No teacher can be involved in two activities at the same time.
              Double decker buses cannot pass under low bridges.

You can't put the engines on the wing before the wing is on the body.

Only one program can have access to the arithmetic unit at a time.

Legal:
No driver may be at the wheel for four hours without a meal break.

Each child must have a minimum of thirty-five hours of schooling per week.

Paint may not be applied in the absence of toxic removal equipment.

Professional:
No mathematics in the afternoon or games in the morning.

Social:
Buses must not use the roads adjacent to the hospital.

Functional:
The number of people travelling on route 7 between 8.00 a.m. and 9.30 a.m., Monday to Friday, is 4350, and they must all have a seat.

Policy:
No ship may go beyond twenty-four consecutive months' service without a major overhaul.

Algorithms: What appropriate method should be used?

Depending on the nature of the criteria and the constraints it may be possible to select appropriate algorithms from the list of already existing managerial sciences. But this is not always the case and it may be necessary to perform some research. What is sad to state, however, is that even similar looking situations cannot necessarily use the same algorithms.

E.g. some pipelines take in all the oil before any is delivered, while others have input and output positions all along the line. Some schools wish to decide precisely which teacher will take which class for which subject while others are happy to provide lists of alternatives. There is no general-purpose scheduling algorithm. Each case must be considered on its own merits. The important thing is to realise that the computer might be able to perform the task better and therefore to study the possibility.

One of the great strengths of the computer is the speed with which it can handle numbers. Thus once we have invented a strategy that will lead to a best possible solution, the computer can undertake the strategy in minutes whereas an unaided person might take a lifetime. Before we had the computer there was little that we could do about the mass of data, but now that we have it we have the fundamental reason for asking the question, should we continue to schedule in the traditional way or could there be worthwhile benefits in trying something new?

In addition to using a scheduling system as part of the daily work you also have a managerial tool in its own right for planning and experimenting. You now have a *simulation* tool at your disposal, one that you have the advantage of knowing that it works. And it is here that the system could quite conceivably have its biggest pay-off. A few examples:

A new pipeline is to be constructed. Your planning department can now experiment with a wide range of different designs, using the system to calculate the throughput.

As the city changes its demographic shape new transportation networks can be experimented with, and their corresponding operating costs calculated.

If the schedule is used as the *input* to a new school design as opposed to the *output* from an existing school, the architect can know precisely how many rooms to construct whereas before it was an inspired guess.

The scheduling program for the computer itself contains a simulation of the particular computer. But this can easily be changed to simulations of other computers as a means of comparing them during the process of computer selection.

I have discussed resource allocation in a little detail, not to belabour this particular point, but to illustrate the general idea. Another example of profit squeezing is the selection of raw materials to satisfy some set of criteria and to do it in the cheapest possible way. The classical example is the chicken-mix problem where we are allowed to use varying amounts of basic ingredients provided certain levels of nutrition are maintained in the final product. As the market prices for these ingredients fluctuate we are in great danger of not producing the cheapest possible set of ratios if we do not have a mathematical method at hand, and a computer to carry out the necessary computations. The method used is called linear programming, and it has become standard practice to use this in operations involving raw materials of fluctuating prices or fluctuating contents. Moreover linear programming is a simple, special case of a more general problem in which the criteria and the constraints are complicated functions.

There are plenty of other techniques already in existence, and details can be obtained from the copious literature. It isn't so much the techniques themselves that are important however but the attitude behind them. You may need the invention of a new one anyway for your particular situation. The important thing to do is not to read up on a set of techniques and then try to find problems that they can solve, but to look critically at the way your organisation is doing things and to try to spot circumstances in which money, materials and time may be locked up more than necessary, given the possibility of examining a large number of options. And having found them bring in a specialist from outside and ask his opinion.

Profit seeking

In profit seeking we are interested in techniques that will help us make better decisions as to what to do with our resources in the future. Should we build new factories? Close down old ones? Redeploy the items we keep in stock? Decentralise the organisation? Enter a new market? Above all, what shall we make or do?

These problems are much more difficult to solve than mixing chicken food, or routing the buses. But because they are so difficult and because they can involve the organisation *in toto,* it can be of great value to use techniques that take away some of the guess-work. Again, let us consider a typical example.

One of the crucial questions that we would like to ask about a product before we actually make it is, how does it work? How well does it fulfil the requirements that it was designed to meet? What does the aeroplane feel like to the man in the cockpit? How much traffic will flow through the interchange at peak loads? We want to know before we build it that it will work and work well. We want to know that it will make a profit for our customers, or that it will last twice as long as our guarantee, or whatever.

The solution to this problem is a technique called simulation. We simulate the aeroplane and fly it a hundred times, seated in a cabin mock-up. We simulate the interchange and send ten thousand cars through it. We make a few changes and try again, steadily homing in on the best possible arrangement, which we can then go ahead and produce in the confidence that it will work.

This is not to say that simulation is perfectly accurate. It isn't. At best it is a good approximation to reality, but even at worst, in creating the model we are forced to examine our potential product very carefully, and this in itself is often very beneficial. It can force our attention on critical aspects that we might not otherwise have studied until far into the production stage.

But a good simulation can be worth orders of magnitude more than its cost, and when people get used to using the technique they come to rely on it heavily.

Before we decided upon the details of a new product we usually want to make some forecast of the marketplace. What gaps are there in the products available today? What would be the effect of a price decrease? An advertising campaign? Are we maintaining our traditional share of the market? How elastic is the demand for our kind of product? Are we evenly spread geographically? Could we obtain a better than average return by concentrating our effort in limited areas? Should we be careful about the timing? And so on.

People have been trying to predict the future since the first hunting party went out and found the first cornfield sown. We are certainly better off today with market intelligence data, sophisticated mathematics and high-speed computers than our ancestors were with the intestines of the sacrificial chicken. However the market place brings us just as many surprises today as the weather gods did in neolithic times. But what we have gives us a little more confidence, and general patterns can be observed and exploited. We have fairly good prognoses of population movements, for example, we can predict the probable demand of airline tickets as a function of price. We have many years' statistics on the cigarette and washing powder markets, and so on. Each situation has its unique pattern, and there exists no general-purpose prediction formula. There is however a wide variety of statistical techniques available once one has decided upon the nature of the problem, and no one ever has enough data with which to work anyway!

. . . . the first hunting party went out and found the first cornfield sown.

A problem that exists in the planning stage whose solution is also usable during execution is that of arranging for the proper sequence of events to take place; making sure that the toilets aren't delivered before the foundations are dug. The solution to this type of problem is called networking theory, and perhaps the best known technique is called PERT, Project Evaluation and Review Technique. As a planning tool PERT forces managerial attention on the details — as does simulation — since every event in the network must follow and/or precede other events, and the probability that a particular event will be forgotten is extremely small. And having once arranged each event as a node in a network, the time and cost of each linking activity can be assessed, hence the total cost of the undertaking and the minimum time that it can be squeezed into.

A PERT diagram can have served its purpose when the planning is over, but it can also be used as a control device during execution, reporting actuals against the plan and allowing management to take appropriate action each time a problem shows up on the 'critical path', the route through the maze with zero tolerance of delay.

These techniques of simulation, forecasting and network theory are examples of a large set of techniques that can help management make decisions about future action. Let it be repeated that, as incomplete as they may be, they can nevertheless be extremely valuable in reducing the need for managerial guesswork, reducing the level of uncertainty and forcing management's attention on the points of weakness.

Costs, values and savings

Profit seeking is a great deal more difficult and uncertain than profit squeezing, but the sky's the limit. With the help of a good technique you might double your profit overnight. There's no built-in upper limit, but the probability of success is lower than in profit squeezing. On the other hand the most you can save in the latter is what the function is costing you today.

It is extremely difficult to give representative figures for

profit seeking — the scope is too wide — however the following
will give you some idea of what can be obtained from scheduling systems as an example of profit squeezing.

Pipelines A department of ten men became one man who
was able to acquire additional responsibilities. The scheduling
process shrank from full-time employment of the department to eight minutes on a mini-computer, i.e. $200,000 per
year became $20,000 per year plus a $100,000 computer,
written off over five years with ninety-nine plus per cent
capacity available free for other applications. Had a service
bureau been available the computer cost would have been
only $100 per month. One has in addition the value of
instant rescheduling in a crisis, involving the value of two
months' supply of oil already in the pipelines.

Factories Here the economies are not so simple because the
companies who use it do so because they have virtually no
choice. In cases of long production runs in which everything
is repetitive and the work force is stable the schedule is produced once and the instructions produced cyclically on the
Xerox machine. However, in situations of widely fluctuating
orders, substantial engineering change and an unstable work-
force, the schedule varies constantly, allowing no actual
opportunity for hand methods. So the value of the computer
schedule is involved in the value of the company, while the
cost might be an hour or two per day on a medium-sized
computer. Here the value lies much more in additional
profit from the factory than in replaced people in the
scheduling department.

City transportation If the main criterion of automatic
scheduling of buses, trains etc. is the cost of operation, the
value of a system is in the range of $50,000 to $75,000 per
annum per bus saved in the peak periods, and $125,000 per
bus saved all day, while the cost of producing an entire
schedule is about $5000. In a recent trial between the com-
puter and a department of expert schedulers the computer
managed to remove four buses from a fleet of fifty-two.

Schools The timetable for a grammar school, high school, college etc. typically occupies the headmaster and possibly an assistant for the best part of the summer, costing, say $10,000 plus considerable fatigue and perhaps no vacation. On the computer the cost is about $2,000. One has in addition the advantages of the better use of existing facilities, delaying the need for more classrooms costing $50,000, and of using the program as a simulation tool prior to the design of new buildings costing millions of dollars.

Using the program

It happens so often that brilliant ideas are put on the computer, embraced in emaculate programs, promising exciting economical improvements for the user etc., but they fail. They do so because no thought was given to their implementation. No plan was created for the consequent changes that the program would bring about within the corporation. Now you can't anticipate everything, and a great deal of the rest of the book is concerned with getting the chain of events right, but I shall mention a short list here by way of introduction.

Gaining confidence

When you have located a target in your organisation that seems amenable to some managerial science, and obtained a technique and a computer program to carry out the dogwork, your next step is to gain confidence that it works. You are perhaps being asked to stake the fortunes of the company on the results of some invisible gyrations inside a black box, and you naturally have a deep-seated reluctance to bet a fortune on an unknown horse. How can you get to know the horse?

Both management and employees will (and should) eye any computer-wrought innovation with healthy suspicion. This should not be confused with reaction, but often is. Before an organisation can invest the success of its operations in any innovation it must have the necessary confidence that the innovation actually works. And while the theoretical proofs are unquestionably necessary they are far from sufficient. No theory can cover every aspect, particularly the human ones. So before uprooting your existing scheduling team, run the computer system in parallel and compare the results. There will be a lot of questions to ask.

Is the input easy to prepare by the working people in actual daily practice?

Is the system easy to operate on the computer?

Is the program 'rugged'? Does it work properly, repetitively in production circumstances?

Does it produce unexpected results? Difficult to carry out or plainly erroneous?

Is the output as easy to use as the input is to prepare?

Are the profit improvements what the man said they would be?

With some of the techniques you can answer these questions in a fairly straightforward manner. For example, before you commit your chicken-mix to the computer, have a computer run every time you order a mix in the customary way and simply compare the economics of the two. Use the same unit prices, but compute (by hand) the cost of both mixes and check that the nutritional criteria are satisfied. If all goes well and the program works properly you will convince yourself that the computer solution would have cost you less, and that to continue by hand would be throwing money down the drain.

But other techniques are not so simply verified. How good is a simulation? The only way of testing the mathematics of a simulation and the accompanying computer program is to simulate something that actually exists. If the simulated results agree well enough with actual results the question then is how different any future simulated situation would be from the tested situation, and whether it contains elements that invalidate the simulation. Not always easy, and often requiring an element of faith. If you can take small steps do so, and place the burden of proof on the man with the gadget.

I remember one particular simulator whose validity no one doubted for a moment. It was Boeing's latest flight simulator and we were using veteran pilots to help us home in on a design. Although the seat and cabin were bolted firmly to the ground we had to keep a bucket handy to catch the motion discomfort (to use an airline euphemism).

Only when you have got the right answers dare you throw out the old method and commit yourself to the computer. Remember, there is no going back.

Changing the procedures

The new system inevitably requires changes in the way the company does its business. For example the scheduling department will probably collapse to one part-time manager and a key-punch girl. The warehouse may have to learn not to fold, staple, spindle or mutilate punched cards. The drivers may have to learn to mark cards and return them in pristine condition to the depot at the completion of a job — and so on.

The new procedures must be worked out in detail in parallel with the computer program so that both are ready at the same time.

Training and assimilation

It is not sufficient to think what the new procedures should be and to write them down, it is also necessary to tell people about them. In short, training.

As you hold your training courses *(before* the system is ready for any sort of use at all) you will have the excellent opportunity of gaining ideas (corrections mainly) from the work-force. They won't understand everything. They will criticise things. They are intelligent people too, and they know their job better than the man who designed the system. So, before it is too late, collect these criticisms and crank them into the system.

But not everyone will be trained in the use of the new system. Some will be replaced and must be assimilated somewhere else in the organisation, or simply somewhere else. If they are to be retained they must also be retrained.

Some fundamental problems

Returning to our introductory discussion on the nature of the scientific method, in the manager's search for methods and equipment that will lighten his load and brighten his path he must be aware that there are some fundamental problems, and it would be well to touch on them in this brief introduction to the idea.

The most fundamental of them is that man the manager is not very much of a scientific species, therefore the closer we come to his nature the more difficult our task. To put anything on the computer we have to acquire a detailed understanding of the problem, and to make it economical we have to solve the problem frequently. These two facts imply the necessity of putting man the manager into the laboratory along with the butterfly, and imply a sufficient consistency of behaviour that will guarantee an economically viable life for any computer program that we may decide to write.

The problem with the first implication is Heisenberg's principle. In observing we change. No one has yet solved the problem of how to investigate the manager at work. If you put an observer into his office, the manager will act some role that may not resemble the true man at all. The presence of the observer will change the behaviour of the observed. A great deal has been written about the species called manager, but it is not in any way scientific, and is fraught with opinion. It does not provide us with a scientific description of managers as a group, and certainly tells us nothing about any individual.

The problem with the second implication is that as circumstances change, or as a manager's attention moves, the requirements for techniques and programs change. Old programs cease to be of interest, while the investment of time and money has to be made into new ones. Computer programs are only *economical* if they are *used frequently*. Moreover, when the boss wants something done, he wants it done now, not six months later after a programmer has perfected his masterpiece.

The creative manager is constantly asking, 'what if?'. Is it technically possible to do so-and-so? What would be the effect on the market if we did this? How much would it cost to do that? He can never say beforehand what he is likely to ask, and when the question comes to mind he wants an answer. He isn't interested in philosophical speculation.

The closer we come to the man and his nature, away from the organisation and its procedures, the more difficult the task. The problem is essentially that of writing a program that can answer questions that no one has asked before. This, in turn, means the necessity for manipulating data in a file so that it can be combined in an infinite number of ways. These are difficult problems. People are tackling them, and some managers today have question-answering programs at their disposal. However there is no general solution, and I do not really know how useful the individual solutions are. One is faced with the Law of Attenuating Honesty:

$$\text{HONESTY} \;=\; \frac{1}{\text{INVESTMENT}}$$

It's difficult to get people to be honest when they've used up too much of the company's money!

Generally speaking, at the working level the computer program comes with the job while at the managerial level it moves around with the manager. As we go up the line, programs become more personal, suiting the style of the individual rather than the objective requirements of the organisation. But economics and the lack of science are making the going slow. In between we have the kinds of managerial subroutines that this chapter is about.

This discussion ties in with that of information, to which we devote Appendix 1, in particular the section about the Holy Grail.

10 The sand in the foundations

We have talked about locating the sources of lost profit in your company, we have tried to explain what computers are and how much they might cost, and we have described the kinds of information taps that are available to your people in their daily work. We have suggested that all this equipment can be incorporated into systems that can unlock some of the sources of profit, but we have skipped ever so lightly over the details of how these systems are actually brought to life.

Indeed there seems to be almost a conspiracy of silence in the industry and the profession. No salesman ever tells you how difficult it is to get anything running on his computer, and few writers ever point out that it sometimes leads to heart attacks and broken homes to make their pristine diagrams actually represent a working reality. This is because the people involved are too busy to tell them.

Computing is like marriage, it's all too easy to get a computer, but terribly difficult to make it work. This chapter describes what the main sources of difficulty are and how to deal with them, and the chapters that follow will treat the tougher ones in more detail.

The dry rot problem

Let's say it again, altogether now — computers are invisible. Computer programs are even more invisible. It is much easier to employ an Eisenstein than an Einstein; reels of film are far more visible than laws of relativity. You can set up all the managerial controls you like. You can count the number of lines of code a man has written, the number of check out runs he has had on the computer. You can examine his test results, but in the final analysis you only have his word to go on. And even if he is utterly honest, his word is restricted by his understanding of the problem as of now. Tomorrow some horrible new detail may crop up that may drastically change the picture.

We may liken this problem unto that of the carpenter who gives an estimate for restoring an old house, and then discovers that it is full of dry rot between the walls. There is a lot of instant dry rot in our programs.

Furthermore, Professor John Buxton says that because of all the changes and afterthoughts that get added to a program, it is much like a twelfth-century church propped up by flying buttresses. So if you think of a program as a heap of dry rot held up by flying buttresses, you will have a reasonably accurate mental image of the typical program.

The definition problem

There is no way of defining completely what you want. There is no way of ensuring that you have thought of every-thing, and no automatic way of cranking your thoughts into a functioning program. In computing, our ways of expressing ourselves are much closer to the stage of cave wall scratching than Shakespearian soliloquising, and there is a long chain of weak links from concept to completion. The customer thinks he knows what he wants. He then thinks he has explained it to the systems man. He in turn thinks he has understood, and thinks that his design both represents what is wanted and is fully comprehensible to the programmer. And so on. It is the only chain I know of in which every link is likely to break.

The upshot is that, at the detailed programming stage,

. . . . a heap of dry rot held up by flying buttresses . . . . .

omissions, contradictions, errors, poor definitions etc. are found that had no opportunity of being found earlier. A design carries no proof of completion or correctness. It is not a piece of mathematics.

The definition problem is a direct consequence of the essential invisibility of the computer, or a manifestation of it. Only in actual running does the design become visible to the naked electron. Regrettably there is no satisfactory way of solving this problem, although plenty of people have produced tools and techniques of varying degrees of efficacy. But as a general strategy, go in heavily for detailed pictures and paragraphs before anyone starts coding, and get the signatures of the people involved that they think they understand and that they agree that it is correct. Furthermore, in each picture colour the least well understood part red and ask questions about the red square every Monday morning. That's what Stalin used to do.

The competence problem

Every profession has its spectrum of competence. There are surgeons who can perform successful heart operations, and there is an English doctor who practices in the bar of a pub. There are architects who design Australian opera houses and there's the chap who knocked my place together.

But probably in no profession is there such an enormous gap between the best and the worst as there is in computing. A computer is a tool, like a surgeon's scalpel, and you cannot assume that just because a person has obtained a lot of experience using it in a particular area of application that he has competence in other areas. You wouldn't want a knee-cap specialist messing around with your brain, and you couldn't expect a payroll programmer to be much help with your structural analysis or vice-versa.

But the problem is even worse than this. Given two individuals experienced in the same computing branch, it is far from uncommon for one to write a program at one tenth the cost of another, taking one tenth the elapsed time. It is unthinkable that of two dentists, one could pull out a tooth in half an hour while the other took the best part of a day. But the equivalent in computing is common, and seems to be either accepted or ignored by management. Far too many companies invest an enormous amount of time, energy and money in deciding what equipment to get, and then only spend a fraction of this on finding the people to make it work properly.

Programming costs increase much faster over the years than equipment costs. As a fair rule of thumb at the moment they are about equal. Invest a similar amount, then, in finding people who are already well experienced in the fields that you want to use them for, and put the monkey on their back to prove to you that they come from the top ten per cent of that part of the profession.

The check out problem

The computer is the most unforgiving tool that man has ever devised. Programming it to do what you want consists of writing lines of code according to a design, and then running them on the computer to find out whether they work. Usually they don't, and the problem then is to find the errors and repair them. This process is called check-out, and this aspect of programming is even more time-consuming than coding.

To check out a program thoroughly and on time requires proper tools and reasonable access to the computer. At the daily detail level it is difficult to plan because you don't know what the problems are going to be until you encounter them. The omission of a single parenthesis will mean a re-run. To manage this problem properly, you should require that a strategic check out plan is included in the programming estimates, and give the programmer either an on-line terminal or a rapid turn-round batch service. Don't force him to wait twenty-four hours to insert his parenthesis.

The criterion problem

When you order a garden fence do you want it to be as cheap as possible? As dog-proof as possible? Easy to maintain? To last a long time? To look nice? You probably have a pretty clear idea of what you want before you make your order.

But how about your programs? Very rarely does management set criteria for the quality of a program. But it makes an enormous difference to the final result if the wrong criteria are assumed by the programmer. Should the program be written as fast as possible? As cheaply as possible? To take a minimum amount of central memory? To run as fast as possible on the machine? To be as easy as possible to operate? To have as many safety checks as possible? To make data acquisition as easy as possible? To produce a program which is as easy to maintain as possible? And so on.

All these criteria are mutually conflicting, but if you ask the average manager what he wants, he'll just say 'yes'.

Unfortunately, we are all too busy to conduct objective tests in order to find out numerically the economic consequences of these conflicting criteria. However, as an indication, we can quote an experiment carried out on two unsuspecting sets of programmers of equivalent ability who were given the same two problems, but with different criteria. One set had to write efficient programs, and the other had to finish the programs as soon as possible.

The results are reported in *The Psychology of Computer Programming* by G. M. Weinberg, and were as follows:

	PROBLEM A		PROBLEM B	
	No. of checkout runs	Mean comp. time	No. of checkout runs	Mean comp. time
PROG. EFFICIENT E PROGRAM	78	1 sec.	60	1 sec.
PROG. FAST F PROGRAMMING	31	10 secs.	27	2 secs.

The penalty to be paid for using program F for problem A is a running cost of ten times that of program E. And even with problem B, if it were hours rather than seconds, the difference in running costs becomes significant.

Another aspect of the test was to compare estimates made after reading and understanding the problems, but before any work was done, with the following results:

	PROBLEMS A AND B COMBINED				
	NO. OF CHECKOUT RUNS		NO. OF ELAPSED DAYS		
	ESTIM.	ACTUAL	ESTIM.	ACTUAL	% LATE
EFFICIENT PROGRAM	44	138	96	152	75
FAST PROGRAMMING	78	58	136	170	25

Here, the problems involved in pressing down the run times of the efficient programs led to a tripling of the computer cost of testing, and almost a doubling of delivery time. Be warned.

It is not difficult to set the criteria. For instance, if you don't intend to run the program frequently, it may not be worth while making it efficient. If you don't intend keeping it for long, or modifying it, there is no point in making it easy to maintain. And so on. In actual practice you will have a hierarchy of criteria, for example:

Must be thoroughly error-checking.

Must be easy on the user.

Must be up and running as soon as possible.

In this case you know before you start that it will run inefficiently on the computer, it will be difficult to maintain and will be about fifty per cent late. You may then, as managerial policy, ask for a version II to be written afterwards to be identical to the user but running efficiently on the computer.

The standards problem

How long does it take you to read a book or write a letter? There are standard costs for painting walls, but not for painting pictures. Similarly there are standard times for punching cards, but not for coding sheets. Designing systems and writing programs is an artistic, creative endeavour, and the creative ability varies widely from person to person, and from time to time for a particular individual. Of course, when a particular individual is writing a particular kind of program for the tenth time, he has a fair idea of how long it will take, but because he is writing a new one, by definition it contains new problems, hence an element of the unknown as far as the cost is concerned. And experience is certainly shared amongst programmers, so that not every program is a completely brave, new adventure.

But the question of standards is so important that we shall devote a whole chapter to it, Chapter 15. It ought not to be your job to decide on a particular standard, but you will want to see that the right standard problems are being tackled.

The language problem

One of the standards problems is that of language, the basic solution to the problem of programmer productivity. Some hundreds of programming languages have been invented. Each type of application offers a choice, and each language has its champions, but there are considerable differences. The more powerful a language, the longer it takes to learn, but the cheaper it is to use when once it is learned. Some languages are well implemented on the computer and some aren't. Some need a host of special typewriter characters, while others don't. A language well suited to engineering may be very poor for accounting, while a language designed for numerical control would be useless for anything else.

If a programmer has the right linguistic tools, he stands at least a chance of coming out on target, but if he has to fight his way through the system with a blunt linguistic instrument, he will miss his schedule by hundreds of per cent. Your task is to find out what languages your technical people need, and then to make sure that they are available in the software supplied by the manufacturer, properly implemented.

The foregoing does not exhaust the list of fundamental problems that together comprise the shifting sands upon which the structure of computing has been erected. But it ought to be enough to scare you, and to give you scope for some intervention according to your style. When you have them all completely solved, I would be delighted to send you the next set.

11 Project initiation — the run up

Having provided a rough basis for estimating the costs of computing, and having hopefully scared you into supposing that the whole thing is impossible anyway, I shall now try to show you how to make it work, including how to get a firmer grip on the costs.

Suppose that by some process of divine inspiration, dressed up in the form of a professional-looking plan, you have decided that it would be economically beneficial and physically possible to put the wheelbarrow design and construction system on the computer. You would like your next step to be to confirm your hunch, but this can't happen right away. The most we can say at the moment is that it *seems* to be a good idea, and that confirmation remains as one of the outcomes of the work. Until we have something more solid to go on, pure theory must be out guide, and confirmation (or denial) won't come shining forth some Thursday afternoon, it will gradually emerge as we carry out the work.

So one thing must be understood right at the start, that since we can never be certain of the result we must be prepared to give away some money. The question is, what is the safest way of doing this?

The answer is to construct an upside-down rocket, to fire one stage at a time and to be prepared to let it crash if at any stage you find that you can't hit the moon. The stages are as follows:

Concept

Duration one day. Cost $500. A senior manager in the wheel-barrow division writes down his idea of what the system should attempt to do, assisted by someone accustomed to investigating and analysing systems: someone from the operational research or systems analysis professions. They should go off somewhere away from the phone and write as much as they can in the time allotted. If you give them a week, they will start trying to provide a solution, and this is not what you want.

Decision mechanism

If they have produced ten pages of problem statement, comprehensible to you and to at least one other manager in your organisation, initiate stage 2. If, instead, you get an outrageous bar bill initiate something else.

Feasibility study

Duration one week. Cost $2,000. An experienced systems analyst and a working-level manager from the user organisation try to create a paper solution to the problem. Some of the time must necessarily be spent with people in the wheel-barrow division, and during this stage it is almost inevitable that ambiguities in the problem statement will come to light. A part of the outcome of stage 2 will be a better version of the result of stage 1. A fact that will indeed be true at every stage.

If you give them a month they will start trying to decide what computer to get. Instead, what you are asking for is a report containing a slightly revised version of the problem statement, a statement of three alternative solutions, with time, cost and value estimates for each.

Decision mechanism

If they have produced twenty pages of problem statement and solution, couched in narrative, pictures and a few numbers, again comprehensible to you and your referee, and if the estimated value over five years exceeds the cost by a factor of ten, initiate phase 3, choosing the solution that appeals to you the most. It is very likely, however, that they will come cap in hand asking for more time. But be warned, the more time you give them, the more detail they will produce, the less likely you will be to understand what they've done and the less likely you are to give it your blessing and enthusiastic support. So far you've had control. Keep it. It can happen that for reasons technical, administrative or economical there is no feasible solution. If so you have spent $2,500 for that valuable piece of information, and you need never spend another sleepless night wondering.

Preliminary design

Duration one month. Cost $10,000. The systems analyst, assisted by an experienced programmer, creates a preliminary system design based on the solution that you chose at the conclusion of stage 2. They use the equivalent of a full-time member of the wheelbarrow department to help them obtain details, but this will really be a series of people, each expert on a particular aspect of the business.

You can expect the preliminary design to consist of a statement of what kinds of device would be installed at the work face, though not the precise makes or models; data transmission requirements; rough file organisation; program specifications, but no coding; testing philosophy but no detailed procedures; user procedure philosophy, but no details; and better time, cost and value estimates.

If you give them three months they will start ordering equipment and writing code. Instead, what you want is a sketch of a blueprint.

What you could get is the discovery that the findings of stage 2 were hopelessly wrong because something vital was overlooked, or an assumption was unjustified. On the other hand what you cannot get is the discovery than an adverse result of stage 2 was hopelessly wrong, since this, in itself, would have stopped the rocket at that stage.

Decision mechanism

If they have produced sixty pages of system design comprehensible to your referee, and containing a short concentrate comprehensible to you, and if the economical estimates of stage 2 are confirmed, initiate stage 4. This time if they come back asking for more time you should treat the application with a little more sympathy than in stage 2 because they are now getting down to detail that should give the final go or no go to the whole project. And the discussion of the reasons why more time is needed will give you some useful insight in itself.

Detailed design

Duration three to six months. Cost $30,000 to $100,000. Again system designers and programmers assisted by wheelbarrow folk, this time carrying out the design to the detail needed for the implementation blueprint. In addition this stage involves deciding on the precise user devices. It may also involve deciding what computing equipment you will want, either to complement what you have already, or as a replacement for it. It will also include documentation requirements, a training plan and acceptance and running-in procedures. This last sentence is of vital importance but is almost universally ignored. Don't join the club.

Decision mechanism

The result of stage 4 must be a blueprint comprehensible to those whose job it will be to make the whole thing work. So before you dare initiate stage 5, the stage 5 team must sign their names to a statement that to the best of their ability to do so they understand the blueprint and agree that they can get it going within the time and cost estimates given. This will almost certainly lead to a battle royal in which heat will outweigh light, and you will be sorely tempted to seek refuge by delegation. Resist such temptation. Have the battle now, and preside over it yourself. To delegate or to postpone the battle to a later date will cost you dearly.

Implementing the design

Duration three to twelve months. Cost $50,000 to $200,000 for people, and the same for computer time. If your bright idea has passed unscathed through all the previous phases, despite your tight management and searching questions, and the economics and feasibility still look promising, you have come to the point of no return. It takes a manager of very cast iron gut or a corporate earthquake to stop the momentum that has now built up. But it must not be regarded as inevitable that the design be translated into a living, breathing system. You may decide at the last minute, for reasons perhaps known to no one else hitherto involved, that the whole thing shall be postponed or even cancelled outright. You might postpone it because you aren't convinced that you have a good enough project leader, or you might cancel it because the board has decided on a radical change in the business plan, or because the official receiver is knocking on the door. But if you do proceed beyond this point you must do so with the full intention of completing the project, even though you have no absolute guarantee of success.

The outcome of this phase is a brand new set of company procedures, some of which will consist of computer programs. And this should scare the wits out of you. You are now about to change the way the company operates. Time-honoured, tried and trusted habits will be thrown irretrievably out of the window, to be replaced by new and suspicious ones that have a guarantee of not working on day one.

. . . . tried and trusted habits will be thrown irretrievably out of the window, to be replaced by new and suspicious ones . . .

In detail the results of this stage are a functioning arrangement of computer hardware and programs, some well-trained people operating and using it, some beautifully written documentation, the initiation of arrangements for getting the system to work properly and evolving it to something very much better, and the glimmer of hope of an economic pay-off.

The work is carried out by a group of programmers, directed and assisted by people from the user department, and if some of the programmers actually hail from the user department, so much the better. In Chapter 13 we shall have more to say on the subject of manning the project, and the creation of a steering team to make sure that the computer people do what's best for the company and not what gives them the greatest kicks.

Decision mechanism

This stage is really complete when the user department is happy with the result. But you won't be prepared to wait that long. The day will never dawn on which you can say that now the system works whereas yesterday it didn't. It doesn't come to life with a bang or even a whimper. It sort of oozes on to the scene, opinions divided as to whether or not it works properly. And your job is to preside over the free-for-all. However, the day will dawn on which a new man is given responsibility for it, the system keeper or maintenance man, and the old project leader is relieved of his post and sent far away on a well-earned rest.

I shall finish this chapter with a remark and a reminder.

The remark

If you find that the time and cost estimates exceed substantially those given in this chapter then you should assume that you are trying to bite off more than you can chew and that the project should be cut down into a series of projects of about this size. There is no guarantee that you can do this, but you ought to have a damn good try. Don't let a project drag on an extra year if you can possibly avoid it. There is nothing as demoralising to an implementation team as a long, drawn-out project that never seems to hit the air, and nothing as frustrating to an enthusiastic, would-be user. To say nothing of the delay in achieving the fruits of what looked like a profitable economic investment. So, as much as possible, keep in mind that in computing projects, even if small isn't beautiful, at least it has a hope of being manageable. We aren't all in the Apollo business.

The reminder

The result of each stage of this upside down rocket is a recommendation to management whether to ignite the next
stage or not. This means budget, so you don't sign off the
budget for the next phase until you are satisfied that the current one has been properly carried out. You are mainly concerned with estimated values against costs. At each stage the
former will have a tendency to diminish while the latter grow.

12 Project control —
how to climb a balloon

In the previous chapter we tackled the problem of how to get from a bright idea to a living, breathing system, and recommended as the solution a series of steps of expanding magnitude leading to a final implementation stage. In this chapter I now want to discuss some of the problems of managing the project in order to carry out those steps.

Getting a computer project on the air is like climbing a balloon. Before you actually set foot on it, its shiny surface looks substantial enough to support you, and its top doesn't seem so far away. When you start your climb however, you find you sink down to your knees with each step, and the going is much slower than you had thought. But in addition, as you struggle up its convex surface, the top seems to move away from you. Then when you get there, it is so flat that you have no way of knowing whether you have arrived or not. But even that isn't all. The very act of climbing makes the balloon roll, and the journey is never-ending. (I am deeply indebted to Buster Keaton for this analogy.)

The question we want to ask ourselves now is how do we manage the long chain of events that leads from bright idea to a working system? To what extent can we borrow from traditional experience and to what extent must we invent new techniques?

Testimony to the effectiveness of traditional methods can be seen in the Roman bridges, Chinese walls and Egyptian pyramids that still stand today. However, even in the twentieth century bridges are known to collapse, and computing projects are much less visible than bridges. So beware!

Superficially the chain of events is similar. An idea of what's wanted. A rough design. A detailed design. An estimate of resources and time needed. The handing over of the design to the fabricators. Fabrication. Testing. Taking into use. And then hopefully a long period of maintenance until the time comes for its replacement by something better. (Except in the case of the pyramids, most of which seem to have survived without any maintenance.)

But there are two significant differences between computing and traditional activities. Computing contains a requirement for precision which leads to a much tougher communications problem, and it has enjoyed (or suffered from) a pace of development unheard of elsewhere in the history of human endeavour. It is therefore insufficient to tell your managers to run things in the time-honoured way. In many ways we have something quite new on our hands, and the following are some of the problems that this leads to.

The pyramid mentality

If you want to build a pyramid, you take a few thousand slaves or out-of-season farm labourers and put them to work cutting and hauling blocks of stone. You eventually run out of working space and you are forced to allow most of them to lie on their backs in the sun and watch half-a-dozen colleagues put the pointed bit on the top. But for most of the duration of the project you have no problem of full employment.

Some companies think you can build computing systems in similar fashion, and one or two have even tried and the results have been disastrous.

The problem is that there is nothing in computing comparable to the cutting and hauling of identical blocks of stone, and nothing in pyramid-building comparable to the mutual information-flow that takes place between the members of a computing team. Each member of a computing team needs to know what the other members are doing. It is very difficult to organise the work so that each can work in isolation. This means that every time you do something you have to tell everyone else, and you probably have to ask them something beforehand. And since the number of two-way conversations in a group increases as the square of the number of people in it, it doesn't take long before the work is swamped by the talk.

Project size

To minimise the communication overhead and propensity for error a project is best carried out by a single person. So if you can wait that long restrict your project size to one man. But if you can't, how large can you allow a group to grow? There is no science of group size, but experience shows that as you grow beyond five the output of the group actually diminishes. Thus, the fundamental laws of project size are:

CHEAPEST – ONE MAN
QUICKEST – FIVE MEN

Alice's problem

Most of the technological aspects of today's automobile were invented at the very start of the automobile age, and since then progress has consisted of fine tuning. Each pyramid was almost a carbon copy of its predecessor. The only changes in the gramophone record this century have been a single reduction in the width of the groove, and its adaptation to stereophony. The fish-hook has remained essentially unchanged for at least 5000 years, and probably much longer.

One wishes this stability were true of computing. If only we could get ahead of the game for once! Unfortunately, the electronic engineers keep churning out exciting new hardware, and in few computing systems do we content ourselves with a small step into the unknown. Instead we make brave, blindfold leaps into the technological blue to try to justify our use of the latest and therefore the best equipment.

Instead of doing this, use the Magic Square method. Write down the two questions shown in Figure 12.1, and the corresponding squares.

Have the proposed techniques and equipment been success-fully used before?

		YES	NO
Has this particular problem been solved before using a computer?	YES	1	2
	NO	3	4

Figure 12.1

Then ask the proposer to write an X in the appropriate square. You then use the table given in Figure 12.2 to find out what to do.

SCORE	ACTION
1	Proceed with the project, provided all the other criteria are satisfied (profitability etc.)
2	Find out what was wrong with the old machine or method. You can get magnificent bargains on the used computer market these days.
3	Find out whether the proposed techniques and equipment are really appropriate to the problem, and if they are, go ahead. They may be the best available but are they really good enough?
4	Promote the proposer to Knot Inspection.

Figure 12.2

The history of computing has been written by an army of unacknowledged knot inspectors running on the spot at a speed approaching that of light. Wave your flag at the passing show.

. . . . an army of unacknowledged knot inspectors . . .

Leadership

The Farrington-Gurney dynasty has been leading chunks of mankind for centuries, so you have no need of reminding that the most important ingredient of success in managing any kind of project is to have a good manager. Nevertheless, all too many projects have foundered because this hasn't been the case. Any other aspect of a control mechanism is only a support of the man in charge.

It is a matter of opinion what precise qualities the project leader should have, however Professor A.S. Douglas says that he 'must be a man of superhuman qualities; a first class technician, an outstanding manager, tactful, patient, humble, persistent, shrewd, unflappable and far-seeing'. But, just in case he isn't available just at the moment, you had better content yourself with going as far down the following list as possible.

First class technician

In this case, by 'technician', I mean 'computer system implementer'. If this criterion can't be met, put the whole idea on ice. At Amalgamated Matchbox you have exemplary management from yourself down to all levels, including George Crudworthy, but at some point we must reach the level where people know what they are doing. To the extent that the leader lacks managerial qualities, these can be made up for by the managerial apparatus to which he reports, but you can't expect technicians from below to come to his rescue, since his failure is their avenue of promotion. Technical crutches are notoriously soled with the skin of the banana.

Outgoingness

And not far below lies the necessary quality of being able to talk to people, both his own and his client's. He needn't be an embryo senator, but if his natural habitat is a hollowed-out log, your systems will be cram-packed with sawdust.

Permanence

The only way to prevent the buck-passing and to minimise the Tutankhamen problem (discussed below) is to keep the same neck on the block from inception to acceptance. The composition of the team will inevitably change as the project moves to the right and different kinds of expertise are needed, but at least keep the team leader.

Leadership qualities

Now you can look for leadership qualities, but not before. The chances are they won't be obviously there, but you must do your share of character building, and undoubtedly this is one of your personal strong points. Give the lad some coaching. A quick trip to the staff college. An occasional invitation to the executive dining palace. Tell him how old Sir Cedrik solved the Shepton Mallet warehouse crisis back in '08. There's far more managerial potential going begging than is generally admitted. The First World War proved this. The countries of Europe would have been reduced to leaderless rabbles after 1918 if it weren't true.

The Tutenkhamen problem

Whatever the details of the way you've got it all organised, you will always have cracks between the formal boxes. And as the project flows from box to box, and different types of people get into the act, it is necessary but not sufficient to have continuity at the top. In addition you must somehow paper over the cracks, and the best way of doing this is to have someone in the current team from the next box in the flow. During the analysis stage have a designer on board. During design have a programmer on board. During programming have a training person and an operator on board. They need not necessarily be full-time, but they must be there long enough to ensure that the consequences of each phase make sense to the next, and that vital aspects are not forgotten.

And the ancients weren't so clever at this either. The problem was overlooked entirely at the installation phase of the tomb of Tutankhamen. The golden walls were designed and manufactured while the rock work was going on, and were installed later by a different team. When Howard Carter opened it up, he discovered that the walls were installed the wrong way round, despite clearly engraved instructions. It was a thoroughly botched job. But even if the installation documentation was insufficient, someone who had been in on the design phase would have realised the mistake and rectified it on the spot.

Pertry not poetry

The fundamental problem of computing, as we have said so many times, is that you can't see what's going on. It doesn't have the visibility of the pyramid. Nevertheless some pictorial representation of the project must be created, and tried and reasonably true methods have been evolved and passed into the realm of standards. The system itself is usually represented by a network of lines and squares, and the activities and events of the project by means of a PERT chart.

Now every important discussion you have about any computing system must be in the language of PERT. Never allow a decision to be made as the result of the spoken word. There are far too many Ciceros mixed up in the computing business. A PERT chart forces the creator down to detail, to get the horse before the cart and to remember all the carts and horses. And it must include everything that needs doing, documentation, training, running-in (and running out, if necessary), acceptance, measuring work, paying bills etc. If properly done, the PERT chart becomes the codpiece of the non-emperor.

The way to use a PERT chart to best effect is to stop the oral flow in mid-stream, jab your pipe at any random activity and tell them you don't believe the numbers. They'll go scurrying out, returning a week later. 'You were absolutely right boss. They're double.' Now you're in command, and the rest is easy. If poetry be the language of love, let pertry be the language of labour.

The weak links

In the discussion of Alice's problem we said that the two most important questions that you must ask of any proposed system are: Are there any aspects of the problem that have not been solved in some way before? And are there any aspects of the technology that are still not fully proved?

What sorts out the managerial men from the boys is actually determining which are the points of weakness; and then hammering away at just those points and delegating the rest. All the squares of a system picture or a PERT chart may be drawn the same size and contain the same number of words, but some are much more solid than others. Somehow you must display the softness. How good are the estimates? How accurate is the critical path? When costing out a new battleship you can compute the exact price of the electric light bulbs from the catalogue, but the cost of a new radar installation, not yet completed, can be a pretty wild guess. We don't add accurate numbers and wild guesses in a proper estimate, and we mustn't represent well-understood technology and current experiments by the same shaped figure.

A square labelled: 'Sort the records in order of person number' represents something far better understood than one labelled 'Find the optimum lathe operating period' for example.

Don't be blinded by the representation. Make it emphasise the differences, not hide them.

Documentation

People express themselves in different ways. It is common amongst painters that they never utter an intelligible sentence. But why should they? They express themselves with the brush. A ballerina expresses herself with her *pas de deux,* and a programmer with his coding pad.

Getting written sentences out of a computer man is like getting money out of an Italian insurance company. Without those sentences, however, the job is incomplete, and what is done is worthless. A system is much more than a polychromatic tray of cards.

So documentation must not be one of the afterthoughts, but must be created as an integral part of the project. As part of the original plan the various documents should be given names and even formats, and as the technical work is done the blankness must be removed from the corresponding pages of these documents.

Politicians are always on about the golden future when man shall live in brotherhood with man. Similarly, programmers leave their writing to some dim and distant point in time when an era of leisure shall ensue. It must be firmly understood from the start that writing is part of the job, and that eras of leisure never come — at least to people who are any good. From your point of view the most important document is the single sheet at the top that tells you that all the other sheets have been properly written and accepted by the people they were written for.

This does not exhaust the list of all the problems that have to be dealt with in running a computer project, but it's enough to get on with. George will undoubtedly create a smart piece of bureaucracy to drape round the whole thing while not forgetting the human details inside, and you will want to follow progress at the major milestones.

13 Project manning —
papering over the cracks

We have described the steps a project should take; we have given due warning of some of the worst problems that the project will encounter, and we have stressed that one of the keys to the solution is to retain a permanent project leader from as early as possible in the life of the project to the day of its acceptance by the user. We have mentioned briefly the kinds of people involved at each step, and the purpose of this chapter is to discuss in more detail who they should be, when they make their entrances and their exits and what they are supposed to do.

Of course at all times and in all places there are differences of opinion about who shall do what and to whom. Who really makes the decisions? Who is best placed to carry them out? How much leeway should you allow the computer people? How close herd should the wheelbarrow folk ride them? How much can you rely on the blueprint and how much interpretation of the blueprint do you need during the final stage? There are no hard and fast answers, and even in your single company you may for one reason or another adopt different strategies for different projects. Nevertheless you ought not to stray too far from the following guide.

The project team

Let us start with the project team. As the project moves from step to step the composition of the team changes and each new constellation has somehow to solve the cracks problem. What did they really mean by this and that? Does this diagram really describe what the programmer is supposed to code? Does this procedure really make sense in the computer room? Can you really expect the users to walk on the ceiling every Thursday? What can you do to ensure a minimum of nonsense and rework? The best answer to this is simply always to have members of the team from the next step attached to the current team as advisors, to ensure that the more outrageous errors are caught at birth. At the design stage have a programmer review each page of the design to make sure that the programmers will be able to understand it when their turn comes. At the implementation stage have a training man on board whose job it is to learn what to teach and make sure that it's teachable, i.e. that the system is easy to use. Include an operator to make sure that they aren't going to be required to change tapes fifty times a minute. Never forget the man from the system keeper's department to make sure that it's an evolvable beast and not a dinosaur.

In Figure 13.1 is shown a typical team composition at each step of a major system.

PHASES

TEAM MEMBERS	CONCEPT	FEASIBILITY	DESIGN		IMPLEMENT	TRAINING	ACCEPTANCE	OPERATIONS & MAINTENANCE
			PRELIM.	DETAIL				
Project leader			A	A	A	A	A	
Systems analysis	A	A					A	
Systems design			A	A			A	
Programming				P	A		A	
Training					P	A	A	
User representatives	A	A	A	A	A	A	A	
Consultants			A	A	A		A	
System keeper					P		A	A
Operations					P	A	A	A

Figure 13.1

An A means one or more people actively working.

A P means one or more people involved to prepare for the next phase.

The project leader

The project leader is perhaps best brought in at the design stage. Indeed until that point one cannot be at all sure that the project is going to come to anything, and it is almost pointless to go to the trouble of finding a man with all the noble qualities required of a leader. This doesn't mean that the effort is leaderless until that point. It means that you are the leader.

User representatives

Notice that there are user representatives present at every step. We know at our peril not to leave a vacuum for the computer people to fill, but that's only because we've had years of bitter experience behind us. In the bad old golden days the user was the last to know. But all that has changed now. Whether the wheelbarrow folk are included as part of the full-time project team or in the guise of a part-time steering team is up to you. We shall talk about the steering team in a moment, but if you want to cover all bases have them in both places.

Consultants

The consultants that a team might need can come from any-where, and may or may not come from the ranks of the con-sulting profession. The point is that they are there only temporarily, and are specialists in particular items that lie outside the scope of the general programmer. Examples may be telecommunications, esoteric equipment, file-handling, mathematical routines, and so on.

Closing the loop

The trouble with architects is that they never seem to be around when the good lady starts working in her kitchen for the first time, or while the husband is out there trying to fix the leak in the brand-new garage roof. Likewise the trouble with computer system designers is that they never seem to be around a year later when the rest of the gang are trying to get the thing working. Too many people in this world are prevented from learning from their own mistakes, and so they go on repeating them elsewhere and on even grander and more costly scales. Please help. Whether it's a new building, a new shampoo or a new computer system, bring everybody back at the acceptance stage. This is indeed the only stage at which you really do need everybody. But it's never done. The only test of a kitchen or a computer system is actually trying to use it. It is here where the cold, misty light of a Monday morning creeps in after the razzle-dazzle, fanfare and the arc-lights have died away. Until now all has been theory. Where's the guy who said that the operators could read the disc labels while they were rotating? Or that the Potts, Nevada telephone system only experienced a single line failure per century? Have their necks on the block until the whole thing works, and then let them take their leave. They will probably have to interrupt some new masterpiece to come back and atone for the sins of the old. That's only a priority problem. But they will return to the interrupted work sadder but wiser beavers.

The system keeper

The system keeper is a man whose existence we have mentioned only briefly until now. Unfortunately he is rarely mentioned at all in working life or in the literature, but his importance simply cannot be over-emphasized. The point is that when everyone else has departed from the scene it is the system keeper, or maintenance man as he is usually called, who is responsible for making it all work. It may be true that it works when the system has been accepted by the using department, but how well? The system mustn't be allowed to die. That is to say, it must not be left in its original shape but must be reworked in the light of experience until it satisfies the real requirements of its users rather than the theoretical requirements supposed by its designers. Of course, if the steps have been carried out properly these two will not vary too greatly, but with daily use, especially by large numbers of people, ideas will certainly spring up that hadn't been thought of before, and if these ideas are to be cranked into the system someone has to do it. That is the task of the system keeper. And it can be a relatively easy task, or an impossible one, depending on whether the design took into consideration the task of making changes after the fact. If the system keeper is allowed to monitor the programming, he will be able to give himself an easy life in the time to come. And be warned, if the system is anything like it was cracked up to be, it will live for years under the care of its keeper, while it may have been only months in the making.

What the system keeper needs designed into the system is something we call flexibility, which will be the subject of Chapter 14. Flexibility isn't something that just happens. It has to be created and it costs money. But if you don't spend that money you will very likely pay much more in terms of awkwardness and lack of ready response to what could be very rapidly changing requirements.

The steering team

So far we have talked about the people responsible for carrying out the detailed work. But who should tell them what to do? Of course, at every critical stage you and your right-hand man have been in on the act, ably assisted by George, but you aren't concerned with the details. You may have made the one-man decision to embark on an on-line order-entry system, but you'll certainly be leaving the question of what exactly an order-entry system is to someone else. Who? Well, in this case the chief salesman, but even he won't have time or patience to get into the details. In the very early days it used to be the computer people themselves who made all the detailed decisions — and often even the strategic decisions. But those days are safely behind us now, and the modern way to control the computer people is to appoint a steering team of representatives of the users.

The steering team must contain representatives of all the eventual user departments and specialities, in particular the chap or girl at the work face. It must remain in active exist-

ence until the system has been bought off and acquired the
status of production.

There is no magic formula for deciding precisely who shall
be in the team or precisely what the team's charter shall be.
Circumstances vary too much. Teams work better when they
are small, but the range of a system may dictate a large one.
The intention may be that the team should be an advisory
body, but because of the personality of some of its members
it may become the major deciding factor. The object of the
exercise, however, is to obtain detailed information and advice
from warm bodies from the firing line, to put the necessary
flesh on the bones of the paper design. If you are putting in
a hospital system don't leave out the nurse or the lad who
puts the stuff on the shelves in the dispensary. Doctors don't
know much about the working lives of nurses, and the only
time anyone sees the dispensary lad is at the annual hospital
ball. He's usually the star turn.

He's usually the star turn.

Now how often should the team meet? Who should attend the meetings? What sort of paper work should it produce? Plus all the other bureaucratic questions. Again, you can't generalise. But you ought to get worried if it hasn't met for the last month and hasn't handed the project leader any paper.

And don't forget that this team costs money. People have to be pulled off their jobs at least to attend the meetings. And they ought also to be spending time with the people they are supposed to represent. This is all part of the cost of producing successful systems, and you economise at your peril.

14 Flexibility

In the previous chapter I pointed out the need for a system keeper whose task in life is to make improvements to operative programs in response to the user's wishes. I said that his job can be an easy one or nigh on impossible depending on the flexibility of the beast he is supposed to lead through the stages of evolution.

. . . depending on the flexibility of the beast he is supposed to lead . . .

We all feel that we know what is meant by flexibility, but in the context of computers there is more to it than meets the eye. The reason why this should concern you is that if you don't pay for flexibility you'll pay even more for inflexibility. Not only in terms of cash out of the window in order to make things work better, but in the less tangible terms of poor morale and downright mistakes.

What is flexibility?

There is nothing as flexible as the mind of a new-born child, or as rigid as that of an old man. Likewise, there is nothing as flexible as an unprogrammed computer or as immutable as today's version of a running system. There is a great deal of loose talk about the flexibility of computers or the systems that run on them, but very little precise definition or guidelines for action.

Firstly, what of the flexibility of computer hardware? The salesman talks of his 'highly flexible computer'. And from his point of view the computer is, indeed, highly flexible. Certainly the computer of today is a much more flexible phenomenon than that of the 1950s. But what do we really mean by that term? What distinguishes today's computers from its precedessors?

Probably the best alternative adjective to 'flexible' would be 'adaptable', and a close second would be 'easy to use', because to the systems designer and programmer the important features of today's computer are its wide range of uses and the ease with which one can couple together all sorts of hardware.

In the early days one had to make the application fit the computer, whereas today there are so many devices available that one can in most cases make the computer fit the application. With only a card reader, printer, small c.p.u. and machine language one had a very primitive tool at one's disposal. No automatic way of converting analog signals to digital numbers; no automatic way of drawing lines, cutting parts or adjusting valves; no easy way of describing processes. One simply had to ignore applications that did not lend themselves readily to punching cards and printing paper, with a relatively simple program connecting the two.

Today the list of devices that can be hung on to a computer seems endless, and putting them to use in the world of application is in many cases no longer a brave new adventure, but is becoming a standard procedure.

There can be no doubt that the availability of hardware makes systems design a much easier matter today than it did in the past, and that hardware can be regarded as being flexible. But what of software?

By software we mean operating systems and languages, as opposed to applications programs. Again looking back at the early days we had precious few aids to programming. One's program was written in a language very close to that of the hardware and bearing no relation to the application. It was accompanied on its way to the computer by a read-in program, or loader, an output program, and perhaps some other primitive library routines to save the programmer irksome details in parts of his program. But the programmer had to do most of the work, not least of which was writing his own programs for reading and writing tape files. And when it was all over, he had to remove everything from the computer, including the files.

Today's operating system does a great deal for the programmer; input, output, cataloguing programs and data in files, automatically putting together programs into a single system − in short almost everything apart from the particular logic of the application. Moreover, the programmer has linguistic tools at his disposal that are fitted to the application and bear little relation to the details of the hardware.

So once again we can say that the business of programming is in itself flexible. Most of the programmer's time is spent thinking about the application and not about the computer.

While hardware and software are provided to the user by a large industry, and have over the years become undeniably flexible, the applications programs are provided by individuals or small groups of people, sometimes with little experience, and it is therefore here where the main problem lies.

We can say that the flexibility of the programmer is pro-

vided by the industry, but the flexibility of the user is provided by the programmer. And if the latter doesn't design
flexibility into his programs, it won't creep in of its own
accord.

The flexibility of the program itself can be considered
at two levels, the ease with which the user can change things
himself without the intervention of a programmer, and the
ease with which the user can have the system keeper do it.

A few simple examples:

a) A program can be written with fixed value added tax
   rates. If the rates change, a programmer must modify
   some of the code. Or it can be written at the outset to
   accept rates as inputs, which can be changed by the user
   without involving the programmer.

b) A file can be designed to contain fixed numbers of attributes of stated numbers of characters, or can be designed
   to accept numbers of attributes and characters as input
   parameters to be supplied by the user.

c) A program can be written to take input from one type of
   device only, or from any kind of input device or medium,
   specified at run time.

If a program lacks the facility for allowing the user to
make his own changes, however, it can still be written in a
nicely-structured way, full of helpful comments so that the
system keeper can do the job.

The question is, how much flexibility should be designed
in at the start? How much is it reasonable to expect the
designer or his customers to anticipate? What aspects might
be very likely to change after the system was installed? Because of change of business or better understanding of the
computer? Flexibility costs money. But so does inflexibility,
and you have the immediate cost of a more complicated
program *versus* the eventual cost of messing about with a
simple one.

The answer isn't obvious. It is easy to blame a programmer
for not thinking of this or that, but to have anticipated a
particular detail could have meant having to anticipate a
large number of general possibilities.

Each case must be taken on its own merits. One must take
into consideration such things as how long the system is

likely to last, how experienced the customer is in deciding what he wants, what aspects of the program are easily and cheaply generalised.

To complete the picture, although most attention is devoted to flexibility in the vicinity of the computer, we must not forget the flexibility of the overall system. We might well put a lot of good hardware to work with programs that are easy to modify, but wrap them up in user procedures that are unnecessarily stiff and inhuman. We far too easily allow ourselves to make rules for using a system that make it easy for the computer people but difficult, irksome, frustrating, irritating etc. to the employee or the citizen. How often do we hear the excuse, sorry but you didn't apply in time and since it's done by computer it's too late now to do anything?

How often is the computer made the whipping boy; the unarguable, inanimate reason why something can't be done? How often is this really inevitable as opposed to inconvenient for the operator?

Income tax returns have to be in by a certain time, but what happens if they aren't? Does the computer automatically issue a court summons? If that is a little far fetched how about automatic non-payment of bank cheques if one's account is empty, as opposed to a report to the chief cashier for decision?

At the design stage it is important to consider the operational procedures from the point of view of flexibility, and to force the user to distinguish between procedures that are truly independent of the computer (dependent on law, other corporate or public procedures etc.), and those that could be hamstrung by bad design. Again, it costs more to be tolerant of human beings, and it is perhaps rather difficult to anticipate all their peculiarities. But the citizen must not become subservient to what he is told is a computer, but what in reality may be a bureaucratic defence mechanism.

15 Standards —

how to avoid heartburn

One of the strongest cards in your hand is the ace of standards. Make sure it is a heart and not a club. If you can be clever enough to prevent the creative spirit destroying your best laid plans, without at the same time destroying the creative spirit itself, you will come a long way towards achieving your goal of controlling your computing people. But let us begin at the beginning.

As with photography, hi-fi, TV and the British sausage, computing started out in a gay, abandoned way upon an uncharted and unchartable path. Everyone invented his own way of doing things. Everyone was a pioneer and there was no pool of experience from which to fish any guidelines. Some people loaded their programs up from the first location in the memory, some down from the last. Some people tested a number to see whether it was positive before they tried taking its square root, while others blithely ignored the sign altogether. Some people put their data as far left as possible in the card and others as far right as possible, preceded by a row of zeros. And everyone was engaged in economising memory space. It was all terribly exciting and we all had that wonderful feeling of being usefully employed in the act of creation.

But most of what went on was either wrong or irrelevant. The creative needles were carefully concealed in program haystacks. We were mediaeval monks devoting our time to beautiful illustrations of intellectual garbage. We were in the picture-frame business.

.... devoting our time to beautiful illustrations ....

The first unconscious step towards genuine creativity was talking about our programs during the coffee break, giving copies of them to each other and gradually making use of what other people had already done to give us a modicum of time to do something genuinely new ourselves. Gradually certain individuals crystallised out as specialists at this and that. Chuck Fendall was master of the art of one-card lower loaders, and it made much more sense to use his latest masterpiece than make your own pale imitation. By the mid-fifties physicists on all floors of the Cavendish were merrily using Stan Gill's differential equation solver without necessarily knowing how it worked.

But you couldn't use other people's programs without accepting other people's premises and adopting their habits. So patterns of behaviour arose which, with the sanction of time (oh, weeks and weeks of it), become standards accepted by the bulk of programmers.

Eventually somebody discovered that we were *de facto* using standards but that they weren't written down and given formal blessing. So the scribes got to work, created standards committees and offered lifelong careers to their members. Standards are a necessity for the economic framework of the world we live in. Camera film, records and cassettes are only possible if they come in one or two sizes. And if you don't like the standard English sausage go to Germany where every city has its own, and get heartburn.

The first question every company has to answer is, what, of all the possibilities, should they standardise on? What are the main areas to consider? The following is not an exhaustive list, but at least gives you something to start with.

Language

You can hi-jack an aircraft but you cannot hi-jack a railway train. When things have built-in limitations there is no discussion. If it runs on a fixed track you have no option but to follow the track. This is the nice thing about computer languages. There are automatic standard imposers. A programmer learns the rules of the game and has no option but to stick to them. The task facing you and George is to decide which game. You cannot afford to run a Tower of Babelgol by letting everyone decide his own language. Most areas of application have a choice of languages, and although there are important technical considerations the choice in the last resort is managerial and not technical. And you have no difficulty at all in forcing the standards because all you have to do is remove all other languages from the software.

However there is a nuance that you should be aware of. Although all the prominent languages have internationally agreed standard versions, there is nothing stopping a manufacturer adding to the standard; creating *linguistic extensions*. Such extensions are usually made to take advantage of particularly useful hardware features, or because the manufacturer feels the standard to be too restrictive. Whichever the reason the extensions are usually limited to that hardware. Thus the programs that use them are not 'portable' to other equipment. If you feel quite certain that you will never need to convert the programs to other equipment, you may allow the extensions to be used. If not you would be well advised to exclude them from your local standard. The choice is between the economics of running today against the economics of continued running some time in the future. A management decision.

The Lord of the Files

You don't let every employee invent his own office filing system, and no more should you let every programmer invent his own computer filing system. Yet this is what has happened throughout most of the history of computing. Traditionally each individual program has its own set of tapes or disc storage in which data is stored in a unique way known only to the program itself; a one-to-one relationship between program and files.

This uniqueness is part of the heritage of the slap-happy way it all got started and it has led to a great deal of inefficiency, inaccuracy, duplication and incompatibility — the cardinal sins of modern life. In particular, the incompatibility of files helped to prevent smaller systems being glued together into larger ones when the need arose. And this led to the need for redesigning and reprogramming (an apparent waste of money although often a blessing in disguise).

The usual situation today is that we find a number of programs using a single file, and a number of files used by a single program. Moreover we often find the need for adding new items to the file and for amalgamating existing files, and we want to be able to do this without rewriting the program. This inevitably points to the need for a Lord of the Files whose job it is to create the standards. And the best way of doing this is for him to create the actual files themselves. To have any hope of survival, the files must all be created centrally, and removed from the domain of the ordinary programmer. The latter's task must be to specify requirements, quantities of data, rates of arrival of data to the computer, frequency of access by the program, and much else, and the task of the files group is to provide an appropriate file and a program called a file-handler. Thus again we have the opportunity of railroad standards without appearing to restrict the opportunity of the individual programmer to be creative.

The aggregation of computer files in a company is called a data base, and the development of data base ideas and programs is now one of the most important features of computer development. A little more will be said about data structures in Appendix 1.

System description

How should a designer describe his design? Every company involved in design and manufacture has to solve the problem of conveying design intent through to the finished product, and company design standards are no novelty. Describing information systems is just a new version of a traditional problem. Standards are needed here so that designers can work together as effortlessly as possible, and so that the implementers (if they are not the same people) can understand what the designers have created, as effortlessly as possible. And much of what is needed is arbitrary and very simple. For example, it is a simple matter to adopt standard shapes representing programs, equipment, reports etc. in drawings. It is only a question of making a decision, and promulgating it. People don't usually object to giving up their old familiar superficialities. It is when you touch them deep down that they react.

In any major system the picture will be drawn at several levels, and there should be a standard layout and a standard way of moving up and down amongst the levels. And connected with each picture will be a written verbal description. There should therefore be standard ways of associating the two, and then of associating them with the coding as it gets produced.

There is a lot of detail here that can only be decided by the individual company. But the outcome must be a 'descriptive language' in which all the people involved are fluent. Let the creative work take place *within* the framework of the description standard, rather than allowing it to be applied *to* the framework.

Documentation

I uttered a little *crie de coeur* in Chapter 12 about the lamentable attitude of computer people to the urgency of writing. Not only must the documentation be complete, accurate, understandable and on time, it must also be done within a well-defined framework because of the wide variety of people contributing to a single entity. A labour of Hercules.

To minimise the misery, and to act as monitor, you can create documentation standards and can employ the services of a technical writer. This is not to suggest that you can standardise the sentence structure, but you can specify the documents that are needed, their layout, numbering, cross-referencing and so on, and can make their creation a part of the on-going project rather than a painful afterthought. If you want to spoon-feed — and you may find this necessary sometimes — hand the technical people the headed, otherwise blank pages and the technical writer a copy of the project PERT chart so that he knows when to expect the contributions. The programmer contributions must be complete, accurate and on-time, while the technical writer adds the understandability and keeps it on-time. It is his task, then, to run up the warning flag if the contributions are late. So the technical writer becomes part of the managerial control apparatus.

A word about technical writers. Don't forget the adjective. They must have enough technical background to be able to find out what the technical people are really trying to say.

Statistical standards

So far we have talked about *framework* standards, but what the world is probably more used to are *statistical* standards. Unfortunately, very little of what goes on in computing is amenable to statistical standards, and you had better be very careful before you go trampling in this particular potato patch.

Probably the closest one can come to reliable statistical standards is in keypunching. Over a broad range of jobs a girl can punch about 1200 cards per day. But some types of punching are much easier than others. Are the cards full or largely empty? Alphabetical or numerical? Are the forms well designed? Is the writing clear and boldly digital? Have the girls been properly trained? A lot of room for deviation from the average. And some girls have inate trickier finger-work than others. So every job has to be costed out in its own right, and assigned its own standard punching rate.

As tricky as standard punching rates are to determine, standard coding rates are much more nebulous. Only over a very broad range of work and groups of people is it possible to say anything about standard rates of writing programs. Ten statements per day, thoroughly checked out, is a figure that gets bandied about, but there is little evidence of any careful measurement. And this figure is per person in the organisation, whether they actually write programs or not, and includes reading, writing and thinking time. So it is only of value as a crude first estimate at the concept stage.

How complicated is the problem? Is there already a solution? How detailed is the system design? How experienced is the programmer? How easy is the language to use? How comprehensive are the checkout facilities on the computer? A host of questions which more or less throws any hope of a standard out of the window.

Be warned that if you make the error of trying to set statistical standards where they don't belong, your programmers are going to want to know how long it takes you to write a letter or read a book. And it won't be any use telling them how long it takes you to clean your teeth or tie your shoes.

It is the very problem of statistical standards that makes programming times and costs so difficult to predict. But even less amenable to statistical standards is the design phase. At least we have *units* of punching and coding, we don't even have this with design. However at the crude stage you can say that a simple system takes one man one month to design, while a moderately difficult one takes six months. However, we all know of systems that takes teams of people years to complete.

Management standards

Is sauce for the goose sauce for the gander? Are you a consumer of your own product? If it's right for your employees to work to standards could it be right for you too? What aspects of your job lend themselves to standards? How about communicating with the computer people? Is it conceivable that you could communicate with them in a formal language? Could you get your fellow managers to do so? You use your native language because you are comfortable with it, but it contains a great deal of ambiguity, and the ambiguity must be removed before the ideas expressed reach the level of the computer itself. Why then not remove it as high up as possible? Not only would this improve communications between you and the people down the line, it would also help you talk to yourself. Unambiguous day-dreaming. Is that a Utopian idea?

You cannot talk in a formal way. But perhaps you could write in a formal way. Perhaps the same kind of syntax and sentence structure that the programmers use on their computer-coding sheets could be used by you on people-coding sheets. I don't know how many people are thinking about this problem. Not many, you can bet. But the problem is being tackled in one organisation, to my knowledge, the Swiss electrical machinery company, Brown Boveri. If successful the idea will certainly spread, but it will be slow going to start with. One can predict that most managers would react pretty violently to the idea of a formal language. But why? Is it because formality plays no part in managerial matters? Or because, by definition, managers are older than technical people, and therefore more resistant to change? Here, at least, is a vast virgin field in which you can pioneer if the idea grabs you.

General standards

One of the principle reasons for the success of the Roman Empire and IBM is the laying down of general standards, and the adherence to them throughout the length and breadth of their domains. The fundamental standards of IBM are their corporate code of behaviour. In the past this has even included singing the corporate songs and refusing all offers of inebriating drink. When you visit them you can't tell whether you're in IBM Japan or IBM Italy.

IBM are perhaps the extreme example, but good, sensible general standards are undoubtedly a means of getting more work out of people. If you decide on the best type of office arrangement for your kind of business, and decree that everyone shall have that kind of office, at least everyone has the feeling that he's being equally treated. If you settle on a single format for documentation, even if the language isn't exactly Shakespearian, at least people will get the impression that their colleagues are doing things in the right way and pulling as a team.

Standards make for mutual identity, good morale and therefore high productivity. And the important thing is that the standard exists at all rather than it aim in some scientific way to be some sort of optimum.

A corporate framework

Finally those aspects of the problem that lie closest to management's heart; organisation, planning and the law. However, although one may be well versed in these activities from one's traditional responsibilities and interests, computing does pose problems that are not generally found elsewhere. The least well understood are the legal aspects. The history of the computer as a legal entity is hardly fit to be printed. But there are reasons for this, and the reasons have little to do with the legal systems themselves. It is quite beyond the scope of any single book to cope with the laws governing computers from a wide variety of legal systems, but the essential problems that need to be solved within each are the same. It is rather difficult to produce neat solutions, nevertheless, as with the discussion of costs, the aim here is to warn you of most of the problems.

16 Computer selection

If you don't delegate your computing to a service bureau you will find yourself trying to cope with the business of evaluating and selecting equipment of your own every three or four years or so. And each time this happens George is going to ask you to sign a bigger cheque, hence the need for you to have some idea of what to watch for. This chapter doesn't tell you how to select a computer, but it will attempt to provide you with some underlying facts of life which you should be aware of in shaping your attack.

There is no science to selecting a computer, therefore there is a lot of emotion. In addition there is always some history, geography, politics, individual relationships, prejudices, prestige and so on. These factors cannot be denied, but it is difficult to treat them in any general discussion of computer evaluation, other than to admit that they exist and even that they can be extremely powerful.

The order of events

The strategy of computer selection consists of getting the events in the right order. That is to say, today's order and the 1950s' order.

In the early days it was the computer that decided everything because it was so limited. The computer itself began at the arithmetic unit and central memory. Card readers and printers were attached to get programs and data into and out of the memory, and eventually magnetic tapes were attached to enable the handling of large amounts of data. And depending on how much memory a computer contained, and its speed of doing arithmetic, one could design limited systems to use it. Improvements meant increases in the speed of doing arithmetic, the size of the central memory, the data rate between tapes and cpu, and reliability. The manufacturers essentially created a computer and said to the world, 'Here it is, see what you can do with it'.

But all this has changed. For one thing the using world has learnt a lot. They have a far better idea of what they want these days. For another, we now have a very rich array of hands-on equipment which we described in Chapter 6. Memory has increased so much in size and speed, and decreased so much in price, that it is no longer a design limitation. The speed of arithmetic is now vast in relation to the requirements of most applications. Languages and operating system features have developed in parallel with the hardware, enabling programmers to work much more efficiently. Data storage devices and file-design philosophies have developed to the point where data-handling has become very much a function of system requirements and not of computer limitations. And c.p.u.'s. are now produced in 'families' which are identical in logic, but differ only in size, speed and price.

In short, three decades of computer development has enabled the user to reverse the order of events. He can now exercise a wide degree of freedom, and even of imagination, in creating a system, and has been liberated significantly from the restrictions of the hardware.

Thus today's order of events is as follows:

a) A statement of user requirements independent of computer.
b) A coarse sketch of a system to satisfy those requirements.
c) A selection of appropriate environmental devices.
d) An array of communication lines and channels to attach the devices to.
e) A calculation of data rates between environmental devices and central storage devices.
f) A calculation of file sizes.

g) A statement of the reaction requirements at the environmental devices
h) An estimate of the amount of computing required per
transaction.
i) Hence requirements of size and speed of central memory
and arithmetic unit.
j) Hence a choice of configuration from the manufacturers,
with prices.
k) The application of a selection technique.
l) And hence a selection.

Chickens and eggs

Because of the degree of vagueness at the outset of this
process, and the frequency of new equipment and techniques
becoming available to the users, the events described above
do not usually take place in a single succession. In actual
practice one may cycle around the list a number of times,
each time coming closer to an eventual configuration. And
the key to understanding this process is that new kinds of
equipment create new ideas for solution, and new kinds of
problem spawn new ideas for equipment. The eggs of equipment produce chickens of applications which, in turn, lay
new eggs of equipment. This iterative process can go on
indefinitely, so the important thing for management is to
make sure that it stops at some optimum point in the proceedings. You can always have a more up-to-date solution if
you are prepared never to have a solution at all, but that
won't bring in much profit. You must cry halt at a stage
where the value of further delay in order to obtain the use of
newer equipment is offset by the cost of a corresponding
delay in improved profits.

The selection process

After you have arrived at a choice of configurations, you
then have the task of comparing them and choosing a winner.
And it is here where we find the least science and the most
emotion, because after all the numbers have been computed,

data rates, prices etc., one is left with non-quantifiable factors such as the quality of the management of the various manufacturers. Thus at this point one runs the great danger of becoming a victim of pseudoscience. The pseudoscientific suggestion is that one can make the entire process numerical by assigning numbers to the subjective factors and adding these in some way to the objective numbers. While recognising the necessity for taking the subjective factors into consideration, one must warn strongly against mixing the two.

Extraneous factors

As I said above, there are a lot of non-technical factors which may weigh heavily in the selection process. Here are some examples:

Historical You have enjoyed a long relationship with a particular manufacturer. You know his people. His people know your branch and your company. The relationship may not have been free from problems, but you have developed techniques for solving them. A brand new manufacturer brings with him a heap of unknowns and unknowables before the fact, and it costs time and money to establish the new relationship. Therefore, provided your current supplier has the equipment you need you are willing to pay more for it than that of a competitor.

Existing computer You already have a computer. It is not obsolete, so you wish to keep it and perhaps order a second one identical to it when it runs out of capacity and for back-up purposes. The task is then to force new systems to operate within the environment of old configurations, albeit with embellishments. In the old days this implied serious restrictions on one's choice of solution, but today most manufacturers supply a broad enough range of equipment for this not to constitute an insurmountable problem.

This factor, of course, is a particular example of the historical factor.

Geographical A particular manufacturer happens to have a strong organisation in your locality. In particular he has a well experienced maintenance crew and a well supplied stock of parts. You feel that he would be far more able to provide the support you need than any of the competition.

Specialisation Although a number of manufacturers have equipment that appear to be able to handle the job, a parti- cular manufacturer has built up a strong competence in your branch and has a goodly proportion of the customers. By going in with this manufacturer you would be assured a development that would keep abreast of the state of the art without your having to invest a disproportionate amount of time, and you would be able to exchange experience and programs with a strong group of co-users.

You may wish to buy from your own countrymen, despite the possibility of more attractive equipment from elsewhere.

Corporate tie-up Your company is a division of a company which happens to own a computer manufacturer. It is either a corporate policy to use their equipment exclusively, or you are encouraged to do so by means of lower prices.

Gut feel From what your friends tell you, what you read in the papers, the appearance of their representatives etc. you have built up a strong preference for a particular company, and it will take a lot of technical persuasion by your people to choose anyone else's equipment.

Patriotism Computer manufacturers are to be found in many countries. You are not forced to buy from the multinationals, and out of pure patriotism you may wish to buy from your own countrymen, despite the possibility of more attractive equipment elsewhere.

There are many other extraneous factors, of course, and these are just examples. However, any selection process must reckon with the human factor, and all we can do is try to minimise the heat it generates.

17 To own or not to own

In the early days of electricity, factories had their own steam-generators and at the time it was probably inconceivable that there should ever be any other way of obtaining electricity. The idea of a city grid, let alone a national grid, was beyond the imagination of most people. And in the early days of computing every user of any size had his own computer, installed on his own premises. Moreover, every individual job was run by someone actually walking over to the computer room and fiddling with the lights and switches and occasionally the fire extinguisher.

Everybody knows that we have come a long way since then, but how far should you go? How far away can the actual computer be? Should it be? To have effective control of it do you have to own it? Or rent it? Or operate it? Are you in a stronger position if you employ the computer people or hire mercenaries? These questions didn't exist twenty years ago, but today the possibilities are legion, and the problem is to get you to realise this and to spend enough time to take proper advantage of the situation.

Like electricity, the availability of computing has evolved, and we can discern three distinct phases. We can regard the first fifteen years or so as a period of *technical experimentation* in which we tried to find out what a computer should be. Although the development that has taken place since 1964 has been much more extensive in terms of the ways devices are logically coupled, their speed, reliability, size and cost per operation, the basic principles were established by that date. During that first period a lot of weird experi-

Are you in a stronger position if you employ the computer people or hire mercenaries?

ments were made, most of which led down blind alleys, and it had all the manifestations of animal evolution, but on a microscopic time-scale.

But, whatever we can say about the early period, one fact was inescapable. You had to be very close to the computer to use it, so you had no option but install it on your own premises, whether you bought or rented. There was very little chance of using a computer down the street.

By 1960 the computer was here to stay. People were starting to take it seriously, and there were already cases where if the computer was down somebody couldn't get on with their job. By the mid-sixties applications were legion, and we can say that the sixties were a period of *managerial experimentation* in which we tried to find how to use it: how to write programs properly, how to operate it reliably and efficiently, and how to organise the whole thing.

But again, for anything like substantial use of a computer, one had little option but continue having the machinery on one's own premises.

And there's no doubt about it, between 1950 and 1970 computers conferred a sort of aura of modernity on a company. A computer was a status symbol, and was displayed in a glass-walled room for all to see. (Fortunately, your visitors couldn't see all the mistakes that were being made, indeed they didn't even know what they were looking at, so it didn't matter.) So even if it had been possible to run work on a computer owned and operated by someone else, there was often a deep-rooted resistance to so doing.

Those days are happily past however. The outcome of the explosive eras of technical experimentation and managerial experimentation has been something so technically complicated that people are now able and most happy to get rid of it, or at least of some aspects of it. And if we want to give it a name we could call the current era that of *delegatory experimentation.* You don't have to be a purveyor of computing to be a consumer of the product. But what can you happily delegate? How? What does it cost? Above all, how do you retain control? Of course, there's no one answer. Everyone's circumstances are different, but there are some very clear questions to ask, problems to solve and options to exercise, the most important of which are as follows:

The branch problem

Computing is, in itself, a branch, just as are plumbing, insurance and shipping. It wasn't seen to be so at the start. Only the manufacturers regarded themselves as the computing industry. But with time things became so complicated, and the users necessarily so knowledgeable, that they too became part of the industry. Moreover, although the industry, to start with, was an exclusively hardware industry, it soon became a software and applications programming industry and even an operations industry. You must be quite clear of the fact that a computer is just as much software as it is hardware, but software doesn't need a factory or large organisations to create it, and so the existence of the software industry isn't so apparent.

The technical complexity of computing as a branch is getting greater all the time, moreover it is much less visible than plumbing, insurance or shipping. You can't see the equivalent of the pipes, the policies or the poop decks.

The question you have to ask yourself, then, is simply can I risk entering a new branch? Now the chances are that you are already in the branch, and got there by osmosis from an earlier and simpler period. But the complexities of computing as an industry may be the very reasons for your problems. In that case your question is, why don't I get out now that I can?

Computer economics

Generally speaking it is cheaper to use a large computer for a short time than a small one for a lot of time. This is true even for hardware considerations alone. But in addition a large computer can be expected to have far more software and equipment-handling capability, enabling you to select from a much wider range of solutions to a problem, and hence an even cheaper solution. Another way of saying this is that a large computer places fewer technical restrictions on the programmer, enabling him to create a solution more in harmony with the problem. Hence a system easier on the user, hence better corporate economics. So if your workload only justifies a small computer you may be better off using a part of someone else's large one.

As a parenthetical footnote we should mention the intrusion of the microcomputer.

The traditional discussion about computer economics centres around the question of having a minicomputer of your own or using slices of time on a large computer down the road (or across the globe) by means of telephone lines. But both computers have an important factor in common. They are both large enough to have to stand on the floor of a room, so their differences are only of degree, not of kind.

However in more recent times the technology has shrunk the computer down literally to the size of the shell or a rather small nut. The processor that stood on the floor of a large room in the 1950s could be carried in the pocket by the mid-seventies. Such a processor, powered by a battery pack, coupled to a cassette tape recorder in the shoulder-bag, and to a small console held in the hand, makes an excellent portable computer and is something essentially different in kind to either mini or maxi computers. Their portability adds a dimension to the traditional comparison of computers, and it is no longer one of economics. Moreover, micro-computers are anyway extremely cheap.

Environmental devices

In the early days the entire hardware of the computer was to be found in a single room. But with the advent of the attachments of the telephone line to the central processor we have experienced a rapid development of so-called peripheral devices that can be placed at the finger-tips of the users in the offices, factories, warehouses, hospitals, on board ship and so on. A properly conceived modern computing system should start at the finger-tips of the user and end there. There is such a wide choice today of such environmental devices on the market, and new ones are so easy to make, that priority should be given to them, over the details of the central computer. The details of the computer are the *consequences* of the peripherals, and the important questions to ask are, does it have the appropriate software to handle the devices, and can it provide the required response? From the point of view of the individual user it is now the computer which has become remote, and the question you have to ask is, *how* remote? Since the computer can't be close to everyone, need it be close to anyone?

The salary problem

Professional computer people are expensive. Or they appear to be so. The really good ones command high salaries. But they are worth it because the real cost of a computer man is not his salary but the computer time his programs consume.

A good programmer can beat a poor or inexperienced one ten-to-one, so it's only the good ones you are interested in. But what sorts of salary level do you already have in your company? How violently are you going to rock the boat if you create a small, highly-paid elite on the company payroll? If this is a problem, a solution available today, but not twenty years ago, is to hire mercenaries. You can use your own employees to specify the requirements, and you should. But the actual implementation can be done under contract by people from a so-called software house.

This can be done, and often is, especially by smaller companies. But you should be warned, there is a drawback. The people who do the detailed design and programming learn a great deal about certain aspects of your business. And they learn it in a new way; in a way unknown to the ordinary employees and yourself. Computer programming forces people to understand things at a minute level of detail never before necessary. But this corporate knowledge, apart from its being embedded in the program, is lost because the people who have obtained it vanish from the scene as soon as they've passed over their handiwork. Had they been employees they would have been a gold mine of ideas for new work relating to the work they had done. But if they work for someone else they may be hard to get hold of. (Of course, even your employees leave. So there's never a guarantee.)

So which is your tougher problem, salaries or corporate knowledge?

The career problem

Can a computer man become chief plumber in your company? It usually happens that when a person moves out of engineering or finance or sales, and becomes a full-time computer man, he is no longer regarded as belonging to his former profession. Probably the only exceptions to this are medical doctor and lawyer. Although whether a doctor dare cut open a patient after ten years of non-stop computer programming is open to doubt.

In most cases the problem is a real one. A man gets a new label, and the question you have to be very honest about is whether you have a career path for a computer man in your company. Of course, computing hasn't been around very long, so we can't expect to find many companies whose president is an ex-computer man. And we certainly don't find them, except amongst computer companies. But in the future, say ten years from now, we ought to start seeing ex-computer people popping up as general managers, taking their place with ex-lawyers and ex-plumbers. After all, by that time they have had a unique career. They will have had the opportunity of getting into the details of an organis-ation like no one else has ever had. They should know the business from all angles if they have been involved in, say, twenty years of creating systems that are the life-blood of that business.

I say, we *ought* to start seeing this happen, even though there's little evidence of it happening yet. But is it possible at your place? Do you see any kind of corporate bar to promotion to the top spot, after you've gone, for computer people? And do they? If there isn't a clear path to the top you are in obvious danger of losing your most ambitious people, and they may be your best people. Not necessarily, but a question well worth looking into.

If the answer is that there is no clear path to the top, and you are losing people because of it, again you have recourse to mercenaries.

The peaks problem

As computing systems move to the right from concept, through design, to implementation, the need for people of various specialities rises and falls. If you employ them all, the question is, how are you going to keep them busy all the time? Your company may be large enough. There may be a solid backlog of good ideas for systems of the future. Or you may have got yourself into a glorious mess, providing a career for an army of computer people to clean it up. (Not the same army that created the mess, of course. They're now down the road repeating their act for the competition.) But if there isn't a full-time occupation for some of these people, again you can man up to a certain level with your own employees, and bring in mercenaries to handle the peaks.

A particular flavour to this and the career problem is this. During the early stages, say ten to fifteen years, you will think of computing as a purely innovative phenomenon. Lots of new ideas perhaps leading to radical changes in the way the company runs and in the way it is organised. But this can't go on for ever. Today the computing industry is a replacement industry. Almost everybody has one. Tomorrow, the *use* of computers will become a replacement occupation. You will scrape the barrel of innovation, and from then until eternity your creative effort will consist of doing it better. And the effort required will almost certainly be a fairly steady one, not admitting of peaks. So the peaks problem may disappear with time. And this brings us back to an earlier discussion, that of system keeping, or maintenance. As time passes the need for the innovator is gradually replaced by that for the perfectionist. And these two may be quite different people. You may indeed wish to get rid of your first generation of computer people and replace them with people of a more introspective nature, whose ambition may well be satisfied in the perfection of their daily work.

The question of size

So far we have discussed good reasons why you should consider having things done for you by companies who specialise in producing systems and operating computers. And you may passionately wish to do so. But you may be too big; too big, that is, in relation to the rest of industry in your locality. A local computing service bureau, large enough to take on a fair share of the local market, may nevertheless be only a fraction the size of computing in your company.

You may be the company in a one-company town; Boeing in Seattle for example. Or you may even be large in relation to the country you operate in; SAS in Scandinavia. There simply may be no naturally existing computer bureau that could take on your work without somehow undergoing a quantum increase in size, and without your work swamping that of their other customers and spoiling the balance of work and priorities that they have been careful to build up. The few cases that do exist of a large organisation subcontracting computing to an outsider is where the organisation has set up the computer company itself — by taking its computing department and creating a wholly-owned subsidiary out of it. There is an excellent argument for doing this. Under these circumstances you have a much clearer contractual relationship between computing and client. And this gives much better control.

Group organisations

Another flavour to the bureau concept, either because there is no naturally occurring bureau in the neighbourhood, or because the nature of the work is too specialised, is for a group of companies in the same sector to band together and create a bureau for their own use. Examples are to be found in the manufacturing industry, banking and insurance. One often finds that companies who compete with deadly earnestness in the market place, cooperate warmly at the support levels, in particular in matters bureaucratic. They can take advantage of economies of scale, the common availability of some scarce expertise, the redeployment of talent and experience and so on.

Facilities management

If you are too big to farm out your daily operations to an existing service bureau, but the glamour has gone and you've learned enough about it to know that you no longer want to be bothered about it, you can invite a bureau in to manage the operation for you on your own raised floor. Facilities management, as it is called, is becoming a rapidly growing business. However in every case you have to decide precisely what you want managed. Just the contents of the computer room? The data preparation? The programming?

Dedicated equipment

Even though an organisation may be using a general-purpose computer for a range of general applications, it may also find it appropriate to dedicate other equipment to special functions, for example the control of processes (oil refining, steel and paper production, for example), ticket reservations, customer banking services, airport operations etc. While it may be possible to delegate all the general-purpose computing to a bureau, lightening an economic burden and removing a tedious managerial chore, there may be nothing to gain in doing so with the dedicated equipment. By definition, dedicated equipment carries only a single application, so there's nothing to be gained economically by someone else running it. Moreover the economics of the computer are subordinate to those of the application, and can be orders of magnitude smaller. In addition the computer may of necessity have to be in the immediate vicinity of the application, and may be attached to a lot of very specialised equipment which an ordinary bureau would not have the competence to handle. So you may well have a split house, running some of the applications yourself and subcontracting others. SAS, for example, run their own reservation system and the systems that spin off it, but subcontract customs-handling to a service bureau who specialises in it, handling customers clearance for a large number of companies.

Selling excess capacity

Perhaps because of the zeal of the vast army of computer salesmen, or perhaps more so because of the inherent difficulty of defining and measuring computer capacity and work load, there is often a considerable disparity between the two, and owners of computers find themselves for a while with a lot of unusable time on their hands. But this is a saleable commodity. Why don't we go out and make some extra cash to help rectify the parlous economics of our computer venture? In other words, the opposite of what we've been talking about. Amalgamated Matchbox goes into the bureau business. And it looks so easy to start with. Some relatively effortless extra income. But what happens later? What is going to happen to your customers as your own demands for capacity begin to encroach on theirs? Or as theirs encroach on each other and on you? What sort of contract have you given them? Did you guarantee to run their stuff for ever? Or for the next five years? Are you in danger of having to acquire extra equipment just to satisfy your computer customers? Are your computer customers taking up more of your time than your sausage customers? Have you deliberately ordered that extra capacity and hired a machine-time salesman to fill it? Have you osmosed into the computing business?

I hope you know what you're doing.

Phasing in

The opposite of getting rid of your computing operations to an outside bureau is using an outside bureau to get started. If you plan eventually to be a large user of computing you can evolve to that state by using a bureau until the economics of performing it yourself dictate so doing. And in this way you postpone many of the tough problems, like how much equipment to get. You also avoid having to free up the space for the computer room. You have to take care of one thing, though. You have to make quite sure that the equipment (both hardware and software) is compatible with what you eventually order. That, or you are forced to order a Chinese copy of their equipment, thus saving you the bother of going through an evaluation process. But go right ahead, you will almost certainly find that the decision to switch to your own shop will stay permanently out in the future, at least if economics are the deciding factor.

The need for back-up

You have control over your own destiny provided your equipment works. And we can certainly be thankful for one thing, that computer technology has finally given us the thing we cried out for throughout the fifties and sixties, but never got. Reliability. Today's computers are extremely reliable. But everything breaks down eventually, despite the best of maintenance procedures. And what are you going to do when it does? Of course, there are break-downs and break-downs. Most of the time you can tolerate the one-hour interruption. You might even tolerate a one-shift interruption provided you had the night in which to recover. But the one-day and one-week breakdown aren't unheard of, even today. All well-ordered computing organisations have a mutual back-up arrangement with a user of the identical equipment; hardware and software. It is usually not sufficient to have *similar* equipment. *Identical* is the adjective. But because of the rich choice of widgets to hang on today's computer, as opposed to those of pre-1964, the probability of two seemingly identical computers actually being so is very small. So the paradox is that although the number of computers has increased vastly, the number of *identical* computers has decreased; at least as a proportion of the total. So back-up between friends is fraught with difficulty and uncertainty. Frankly it doesn't work well. But back-up between service bureaux can be quite another matter. Their very existence ought to depend on it. If they can't make guarantees to their customers they ought not to have customers. So it could well be that back-up is your ultimate reason to hand over to a bureau.

How to control the bureau

If you run your own shop you at least have the feeling that you're in charge. The machine may break down while the payroll is being run, or the operators may go on strike, but outside such acts of God, the day will certainly dawn on which you, with the help of your managers, will have a well-tuned computer run by well-trained people according to well-written documentation. It won't start out that way, but you'll get there some time. But can you have the same degree of control over a bureau? How many other customers do they have today? How many keen salesmen are out banging on the doors of new customers? How much time do you need each day? How often? What is the bureau's total as a fraction of twenty-four hours? Do they have enough slop to recover from a short breakdown? What sort of guarantee are they giving you? (What sort of guarantee could you give yourself?) All these questions must be thoroughly investigated, and the answers cranked into a tough contract. If you are taking anything like full advantage of today's computer technology you will be using it to support vital elements of your company; manufacturing, sales, design and so on. If the computer doesn't deliver, your company may stop working. The bureau must understand this and face up to the responsibility legally. If they aren't prepared to do this you daren't subcontract computing, and this whole discussion becomes academic.

Advice

This chapter has described what seems to be the most important factors to consider in deciding whether or not to use a service bureau. You can't make an absolute case. Everyone's circumstances are different. The factors are economics, corporate know-how, local conditions, corporate size, the nature of your business, and so on. And still today a lot of people, management as well as technical, like the fun of having a computer. And the career. Computers have created a lot of careers. (Have you ever stopped to think what these hordes of computing people would have done with their lives if the computer hadn't been?) But these things don't necessarily contribute to the economics of the situation (at least not positively). In the old days the choice didn't exist. It does today, so my advice is genuinely to sound out the service bureau market place and play the competition, either before you give serious thought to running your own shop, or to get rid of the shop that has mushroomed on your own floorspace.

18 The computer and the law

a   A solid contract

Few lawyers understand computing and few computing people understand the law. Your past experience has caused you to learn something of the one, and you are in the process of trying to learn something of the other, so with a little bit of luck you won't find it too hard to gain control of the computer contract negotiations. Indeed you daren't do otherwise, because if things go wrong they can go wrong very badly, even to the extent of destroying your company. But even if things aren't that bad, you can still be forced into a situation into which the computer becomes your main concern while you perform a rescue operation. And all because you didn't harvest a little managerial time at the right moment.

And while you are asserting yourself over George and your lawyer, you grab the computer salesman in the same fell swoop.

To give you some idea of what's at stake if you don't, let's just listen in to a case that's about to begin in which Amalgamated Matchbox has made the mistake of suing Hairy Hardware Inc. for breach of contract.

Scene: Courtroom
Characters: Judge O'Solomon
          Counsel for the Plaintiff, Amalgamated Matchbox (AM)
          Counsel for the Defence, Hairy Hardware Inc. (HH)

Judge: Will the Counsel for the Plaintiff please state his case.

AM: Your Honour, my client is not satisfied with his computer, purchased from Hairy Hardware Inc. two years ago, and wishes to return it for the full price paid plus damages amounting to the cost of programming and operating it during the two-year period, plus the estimated lost profit.

Judge: What has the Counsel for the Defence to say to this suit?

HH: My client denies that any dissatisfaction with the computer is the fault of his company, and moreover is counter-suing for damaged reputation, Your Honour.

Judge: (to HH): For the edification of this court would Counsel please explain what he actually supplied the Plaintiff.

HH: My client supplied a computer, Your Honour.

Judge: Would it be possible to state more explicitly what the computer consisted of? I imagine there are computers and computers.

HH: (reading from a long sheet of paper): Your Honour, the computer consisted of a central processing unit of 256K words of memory, an arithmetic unit capable of executing 2 million additions per second, sixteen multiplex channels, four selector channels, two card-readers, four printers, one card-reader control unit, one reciprocating lurgi extractor . . .

Judge: (interrupting): Hold hard there now Counsel. That's enough. Tell me, how many items do you have on that list?

HH: 137, Your Honour.

Judge: Then instead of reading them out perhaps you would be so good as to pass the list to the Counsel for the Plaintiff.

Judge: (to AM): Do you agree that this list describes the computer in question?

AM: Yes, Your Honour, this is indeed what was ordered.

Judge: Was it delivered in its entirety?

AM: Yes, Your Honour.

Judge: And that was the total commitment of the supplier?

AM: No, Your Honour. The list only covers the extent of the hardware. However in addition the Defendant had also to supply the necessary software.

Judge: (to HH): Does this statement accord with the opinion of the Defendant?

HH: It does, Your Honour. The software was supplied by my client's wholly-owned subsidiary, Sporty Software Inc.

Judge: Pray tell the Court what the software consisted of.

HH: The software, Your Honour, consisted of an operating system, ABSYS 3, allowing interactive foreground and batch background; three compilers, TWITRAN, a simple language for engineers, GOBALD, a simple language for accountants, and KO-KO, a self-executing language for software writers; handlers for all the hardware devices; and a file-handling system called CELLCAKE.

Judge: And was this delivered with the hardware on the agreed date?

HH: It was, Your Honour.

Judge: Does Counsel for the Plaintiff agree?

AM: I do, Your Honour. My client is not complaining that the hardware and software were not delivered on schedule. The software as delivered agreed with the written descriptions supplied by the Defendant. What my client is suing for is that the computer did not perform as predicted by the Defendant.

Judge: I don't understand. What is meant by the verb 'perform' in this context?

AM: The computer did not carry out the functions required by my client with the required speed and at the specified cost, Your Honour.

Judge: (to HH): As a point of explanation, could you please tell the Court whether it is the hardware or the software of a computer that carries out the functions required by the user. Which was at fault in the opinion of the Plaintiff?

HH: Your Honour, both hardware and software are involved in carrying out these functions, but both are under the direction of so-called application programs. The application programs speak to the software, and the software speaks to the hardware.

Judge: And the hardware speaks to God, I suppose.

HH: In a sense, yes, Your Honour. At the hardware level we are down to fairly fundamental physics and the speed of light.

Judge: It appears that you have introduced a new element into the picture. What is an application program?

HH: Well, Your Honour, in that the hardware and software supplied by a manufacturer to two customers may be identical, it is the application programs that make them different. It is the application programs that cause the computer to carry out the wishes of the user.

Judge: In this case, who was responsible for creating the application programs?

AM: My client, Your Honour.

Judge: Then am I to understand that beyond the delivery of the hardware and software the Defendant had no responsibility for the success of the computer?

HH: Naturally, Your Honour, my client carried out a great deal of customer training. He provided expert consultation when required, and has maintained the equipment in an excellent state of reliability. But apart from that it is the responsibility of the customer to make the computer carry out productive tasks. If you'll pardon my facetiousness, Your Honour, it is my client who delivers the tools, and his customer who carries out the job.

Judge: (to AM): Is Counsel for the Plaintiff in agreement with this point of view?

AM: In so far as the case has been stated, Your Honour, it was my my client's employees who wrote the application programs. But when the programs were run on the computer they were far too slow. The computer was not fast enough to enable the programs to carry out all their required tasks in the time available.

Judge: But whose fault was that?

AM: In the opinion of my client, Your Honour, it was the fault of the Defendant for recommending a type of computer that was not sufficient to the task.

Judge: Was the Defendant aware of the nature of the task before the computer was ordered?

AM: A fully documented statement of the application was given to a number of manufacturers, Your Honour, and the Defendant won a competition for supplying the computer.

Judge: Does this accord with the view of the Defendant?

HH: Yes, Your Honour. My client was fully aware of the nature of the application, but he stands by his original recommendation as to choice of equipment.

Judge: But how can he do this if the computer is demonstrably below par?

HH: With all due respect, Your Honour, it is not the computer that is below par, but the capability of the Plaintiff's employees to use it. He used insufficiently experienced people, Your Honour.

Judge: Careful, Counsel, you are out on the thin ice of human competence. A very controversial factor, scarcely amenable to objective measurement.

HH: Begging your pardon, Your Honour, but is computer competence any more measurable than human competence?

Judge: I should certainly hope so. A computer is a machine and machines are all subject to measurement, are they not? Cranes are built to lift stated weights, buses to carry stated numbers of passengers. Is this not the same with computers? What yardstick is the Plaintiff using to measure the output of his computer?

AM: The application that my client is using the computer for, Your Honour, is ordering goods from his warehouses. The computer contains an up-to-the-moment picture of the contents of the warehouses, and every customer order is transacted by means of the computer. In short, Your Honour, the computer, to my client, is a warehouse control and ordering machine. To another customer it might be an engineering computation machine or a financial control machine. Indeed one and the same physical computer might be a number of these machines simultaneously. But as a warehouse control and ordering machine, my client requires a throughput of five transactions per second, Your Honour.

Judge: Do you mean to tell the court that it is possible for a computer to be analogously a crane and a bus simultaneously?

AM: Yes, Your Honour.

Judge: And that this implies that its output has to be measured in totally different ways?

AM: Yes, Your Honour.

Judge: Then a computer cannot be regarded as a machine in the
         traditional sense?

AM: No, Your Honour. The kinds of machine you refer to are
         mechanical objects, while the computer is a *logical* object, and
         there exists no such thing as a logical unit of measurement.
         We therefore have to define the computer in terms of the
         productive transactions it is capable of per unit of time.

Judge: And you are telling the court that your client's yardstick is
         warehouse transactions, and that this ought to be five per
         second?

AM: Yes, Your Honour. A minimum rate of five per second when
         all enquiry stations are busy.

Judge: And what rate is he obtaining?

AM: One, Your Honour.

Judge: In other words, the computer is operating at one fifth the
         required speed.

AM: Yes, Your Honour. And the consequence of this is a long
         queue of transactions at the busy times of the day, poor
         response to the customers and an inevitable loss of business.

Judge: And what does the defendant have to say to this charge?

HH: Your Honour, my client was indeed informed that the
         minimum rate would have to be five transactions per second.
         Moreover he has supplied a computer which, competently
         programmed, has the capability of providing this rate.
         However, Your Honour, in addition to my client's claim of
         poor technical work, he is also of the opinion that the
         transactions actually programmed are not those described in
         the original specification. That, indeed, they are far more
         ambitious than initially envisaged. My client therefore absolves
         himself from all responsibility for the lack of apparent
         capability of the computer.

Judge: I think the point has arrived in the proceedings where we
         must take out the contract. What is specified in the contract
         regarding the capability of the computer?

HH: Nothing, Your Honour. The contract itself is for hardware
         only.

AM: I beg to differ, Your Honour. It is true that the document containing the signatures is for hardware only, but this is not the only part of the contract. In addition there are the software manuals written by the defendant, and the problem specification written by my client.

Judge: Does the Counsel for the Defence agree with this interpretation of the constitution of the contract?

At this point I think we shall creep stealthily away . . . .

HH: No, Your Honour. The contract consists solely of the hardware document. The other pertinent documents are only support material. The software is always subject to modification, and indeed is in a perpetual state of development, while the problem specification was a *precursor* to the contract, *enabling* the contract to be consummated, but not constituting part of it.

AM: I beg to differ, Your Honour. Since the application programs and the computer together constitute the *physical* entity of the contract, their descriptive documents must together constitute the legal entity. Moreover, the fact of the perpetual state of development of the software is irrelevant since it is not incumbent upon my client to accept new releases after the version that was delivered with the hardware.

At this point I think we shall creep stealthily away and leave the poor old judge to it. His task is a hopeless one, of course, and he will have to dismiss the case. From this point on, the more he asks the more bewildered he will get, and it won't be long before he won't know what to ask. Neither counsel has a good case. Their respective clients did not do enough work at the contract stage, and have not worked closely enough since. Thus both are losers. Amalgamated Matchbox have lost money and will continue to do so, while Hairy Hardware are in great danger of losing their reputation and will have to come to their customer's rescue, whether they deserve it or not. The case will, *de facto*, get settled out of court, and it would have been cheaper to have avoided the court altogether.

The points of legal weakness were:
1. What comprised the formal contract?
2. A document setting out clearly the respective responsibilities.
3. A procedure for formally accepting the computer.
4. Whether the application was sufficiently well defined in the original tender.
5. A means of ensuring that the customer used sufficiently competent people.

Both sides are to blame, a manufacturer dare not let a customer make a mess of things for fear of its reputation and future business, while a customer cannot expect a bunch of warm bodies to make a computer work effectively.

Your managerial task is to ensure that the manufacturer's salesman, your own computer manager and your company lawyer have a watertight legal arrangement before you sign the contract. All the worst possible results must be contemplated beforehand, and procedures, written down to cover every case, must be included in the contract. Most contracts are signed in the light-hearted assumption that all will go right. If you, instead, assume that all will go wrong, you may have cause for a faint smile three years from now. But, whatever you do, never go to court.

19 The computer and the law

b A chain of possible disasters

The contract for the purchase or rent of a computer is the single most important legal item for your attention, but it isn't the only one. If you manage to get a computer up and running, and start to put some really worth-while applications on it you will become vulnerable to a series of threats which you must be aware of, even though I should say at once that you will not be able to defend yourself against them as effectively as you can the other things that you get up to.

The fundamental difficulties that the law has with the computer are its invisibility and the lack of a universal, objective means of measuring it. You can't see it and you can't measure it. How, then, can it take its place in court? Let us examine these problems in a bit more detail and see some of their legal consequences.

The unit problem

As became evident in court in the previous chapter the root problem is the lack of units. There is no absolute and universal way of describing or measuring computing. Thus at the core of every contract lies something that must be taken on trust, with the consequent danger that it will be argued about, possibly in court. Although we may be able to fill the contract with all sorts of objective measurements, the size of the central memory, the weight of the cabinets, the power requirements, the date of delivery of the hardware, as well as the colour of the operator's chair, the most important features, throughput and reliability, contain factors of arbitrariness.

Throughput has to be defined for every contract, and its measurement must be in terms of a fixed set of work which we call a bench mark, while reliability is measured in terms both of frequency of failure and total time of failure over an agreed period. It cannot be one hundred per cent, and at the contract negotiation stage acceptable figures must be agreed to.

But after acceptance of a computer there is always a possibility for both throughput and reliability to degrade, and both are therefore candidades for litigation. Throughput may *appear* to degrade because the work mix changes, or may actually degrade because of new features in the operating system. While reliability may degrade because of poor preventative maintenance, untested engineering changes, fluctuations in the power supply, a substandard supply of magnetic tapes, and many other reasons.

These things must be properly understood at the contract negotiation stage, and provided for as exhaustively as possible in the contract. However they cannot be removed entirely from the realm of opinion, and will always be a source of potential dissatisfaction. It is therefore vital to keep a full history of the behaviour of the computer after acceptance, documented in a form suitable in case of eventual litigation.

Application programs

If your company is writing its own application programs it is hardly likely that legal considerations will enter the picture. But if you are subcontracting the work to an outside company a contract must be written. And this type of contract is even more nebulous than that for the purchase of a computer. In addition to the problem of units is the problem of defining the program to be written. There is no scientific way of specifying a program, and no automatic way of proceeding from a specification to a finished product. Indeed, there is no way of knowing whether the product is actually finished. The customer has no way of saying precisely what he wants, and the supplier has no way of proving that he has met the requirement. (In addition is the non-legal problem that the customer doesn't really know what he wants in many cases.)

By means of narrative, mathematical expressions, diagrams and numbers a customer may do his best to express himself, and the programmer may well think he understands what has been written. The next step is for the programmer to supply a time and cost estimate, and this brings up the question of whether the contract is for a fixed price or not. A programmer would be extremely foolish to accept a fixed price for a job which was vastly different from anything he had ever done before, while the customer would be equally foolish to hand the programmer a blank cheque. Hence negotiation. The important thing is that the contract specifies precisely the terms, but there will always be a danger that either party, or both, are putting their signatures to something that they *think* they understand, but that the light of later experience shows otherwise. Perhaps all such contracts should contain a clause stating that the contract is null and void if problems of specification are discovered during implementation.

The problem of proving completion lies in the difficulty of testing all possible states of the program, at least before the program is taken into productive use. Programs contain errors, and some errors can pop up months after the program was accepted, paid for and taken into daily use. The following newspaper clipping from *Computing,* 2 August, 1973 is a typical such specimen.

SYSTEMS BREAKDOWN BRINGS USER CHAOS

Temporary chaos came to a large number of installations throughout Europe on 19 July when many users found that Grasp, the spooling package from Software Design, would not start up.

The package is used by over 200 IBM DOS customers in Europe.

The problem was rectified initially by starting the system using an earlier date.

The reason for the failure of Grasp in some installations and not in others remains obscure. The only clear fact is that 19 July is day 200 in the Julian calendar and this could be in some way at the root of the problem.

Keith Piper, technical director of Software Design, avoided the implication that there was a 'bug' in Grasp by stating. "All I can say is that we have not changed anything in Grasp to cure it.'

He added: 'Grasp customers have all been informed of how to remedy the situation — by changing certain supervisor options which were determined to be relevant.'

Users who were affected by the problem generally regard it as one of the difficulties which occasionally beset any computer installation.

Completion cannot be proved, so a legal test must be specified at the *negotiation* stage, and when the program has passed this test it must be regarded as legally complete even though there is every possibility that it contains an error. And the contract must specify who does what and who pays whom for error correction after acceptance.

However not all programming is done in this way. There is a growing business in the use of existing programs. And here the customer can do all the testing he wants, to satisfy himself that a program behaves as advertised, before signing the dotted line. He may require some modifications, but this is usually a minor affair in comparison with creating a complete program.

Program ownership

The next question that you will want to ask is, when a program is finished who owns it? This, too, must be clearly specified in the contract. Both customer and supplier have copies of the program, and the latter may well want to try to sell it again to other customers. But such customers may be competitors of the original customer, and the program may contain competitive features. If, however, the customer allows the supplier to market the program further, should the customer be paid a royalty in the hope of regaining his fee? Indeed it may be agreed beforehand that the customer pay a price lower than cost against the marketability of the program. Alternatively the customer may pay a higher price for the right to restrict its use elsewhere for a period of two years, say.

But what about the experience gained in writing the program by the company doing it? Or by the individuals concerned, who may leave their present employment and take their experience elsewhere? Tough legal problems that at least need airing each time.

Security of programs and data

In discussing the question of ownership I pointed out that a program could contain competitive features. Moreover, it also has a value internally to the user organisation, and could be usable by another organisation even if it did not represent a competitive advantage. Thus there is always a danger of someone stealing your programs. Now if someone steals your car you know it by the space created in your executive parking area, and you can give a description of it to the police. But if someone steals your program you still have it. You may not know that it has been stolen, and even if you do you may have a tough time proving it. But stealing the program itself is not sufficient. A potential user needs detailed information about how to use it, how to train people in its use, how to get it running and how to improve it. He needs a lot of detailed documentation and his safest bet would be to employ the services of your man who knows the program best. Thus you are most vulnerable to program stealing by your own employees, and this represents a legal situation between you and them that is a bit different to that of stealing wheelbarrows. And even if an employee leaves without taking anything away in his brief case, he can remember what he did, at great expense to you, and repeat it for a new employer at a fraction of the price.

One is not helped much here by the copyright or patent laws because it is so difficult to define a program in legal terms, and to prove contravention.

No general solution has been forthcoming to this problem and every case must be considered on its own merits. But what you can be strongly advised to do is to review the contractual circumstances of employees engaged in computer work.

In addition to programs are data. We know that there is a great deal of industrial espionage being carried out, and we create much of our formal corporate information with the computer; financial, design, planning, marketing, and so on. Information sitting on magnetic tape can very easily be printed on someone else's computer. The penalty for stealing $20 worth of magnetic tape is insignificant, but the value of the data sitting on the tape can be millions. The question is, can you prove this to the judge? Is a magnetic tape legally identical to sheets of paper containing the same information? This question has never been settled.

However one way of determining the value of a stolen reel of tape is to use it for blackmail. This has been done to public knowledge once, and the value was in the millions.

The only real safeguard against stealing data, be it on paper or on tape, is to create stringent procedures within the organisation. And this also applies to simple loss of data. In theory one can always recreate it, but in practice this can be a tedious process, involving lengthy delays. There is no substitute for a rigorous procedure in which all important data tapes are removed from the building and stored in a fire-proof vault for a minimum period of time.

Subliminal stealing

A rather sad aspect to all this is that you can be robbed by your own programmers. And they can do this without anything appearing to be wrong. Nothing seems to be missing.

The accounts balance. Money leaks out but you aren't even aware of it. There may be undetected cases going on at this moment, but at least one programmer has been convicted of stealing *inside* the program itself. In this well-known case he inserted a piece of coding in a program which transferred to his account the small, ignored amounts resulting from rounding to the nearest dollar or cent.

I must hastily leap at this point to the defence of the programming community, to stress that this was an out-and-out exception. Most programmers are scrupulously honest people, hard-working, enthusiastic and loyal. They don't always produce the right answers, but that's not because they don't try! Programs should have built-in audits, but there's no guarantee of completion, and anyway, in the final analysis, who audits the auditors? As Groucho Marx once put it, 'I've got my first cousin watching the safe, and my second cousin watching my first cousin'.

Insurance

Having mentioned some of the threats, let us now ask the question, what can you insure against? Can you sue a computer? Consider the following horror-story that appeared in the London *Daily Mail* on 9 October, 1972.

COMPUTER PUTS PAID TO BOOMING BUSINESS

It made errors, so bills went unpaid.

For fifty years a firm thrived as a staff of clerks kept the accounts with the aid of leather-bound ledgers. But after a computer took over last year, the firm's financial affairs became chaotic and eventually the company crashed. Now the computer has been blamed by the managing director for the firm's failure. The computer started operating in April 1971, at the head office in Stratford, London, E., of shipping agents Armfields International. Little more than a year later the firm collapsed, owing £544,531, and throwing more than 140 people out of work. 'The computer went wrong from the word go,' said managing director Mr Peter Armfield, at a creditors' meeting in London. 'In sorting out errors, other costing errors cropped up.' The company cash flow slumped because customers refused to pay when they received inaccurate accounts. 'Clients took advantage of the situation', said Mr Armfield. Without money to pay its own bills, the company's suppliers either restricted or withdrew credit facilities. 'Mechanical and programming difficulties created extensive accounting disorder', said Mr Alfred Davis, a chartered accountant appointed receiver by Lloyds Bank. 'The debtor and creditor ledgers were affected by the computer difficulties, and the agreement of accounts became impossible.'

ACUTE

Financial experts were called in by the company to sort out the problems, but on May 23 this year the company's headquarters were gutted by fire and the computer was completely destroyed. Mr Davis said that the fire made the company's difficulties more acute. All that was left of the accounts section was some mutilated ledger cards. Customers disputing their accounts could not be challenged. It now seemed that the company had lost about £300,000 in the last year of its life. Mr Armfield, who is owed about £20,000, added: 'I am the largest unsecured creditor.' More than 500 creditors are involved in the crash.

What could Mr Armfield have done? His options were two-fold; taking steps to prevent the disaster, and insuring against it, should it happen. The former is what this book is all about, proper organising, proper planning, proper documentation, proper control. But what about the latter? At a very minimum he needed about half a million pounds to pay off his creditors, and he would still be left without a business. Where do the various agents stand in a case like this?

The manufacturer's stand is quite clear. His responsibility ceases with acceptance of the computer and its maintenance contract by the user; that is, before the user has had any opportunity to do any harm. What the user does with the computer afterwards is his affair. A car salesman is not responsible if you violate the traffic laws.

The system designer's stand is that he created a set of diagrams and explanations that management agreed was what they wanted.

A car salesman is not responsible if you violate the traffic laws.

The programmer's stand is that his program survived all the tests that management specified before it was taken into use.

The operators' stand is that the data was properly key-punched and verified and that the programs were run according to the procedures agreed to by management.

The accounts department couldn't know that the output was in error before bills were sent out, and they found it difficult to confirm or deny complaints of errors sent back from the customers.

And so on. An insurance company would have no one to turn to. So while it would insure against tangible disasters like fire or flood, it is hardly likely to underwrite something as intangible as an incompetent network of apparently competent agents. So indeed Mr Armfield had no second option. He blamed the computer, but he could never have succeeded in bringing an action against it.

Confidentiality

Although this does not exhaust the list of possible legal aspects, I shall finish this chapter with a short discussion of the question of confidentiality. This problem has created a great public stir, partly because there are some genuine dangers, and partly because the press plays it up, sometimes without a full grasp of the facts.

The fundamental fact is not that we now have the ability to handle information about people for the first time. The Romans probably had their slave lists. The fact is that we can now handle this information more efficiently than ever before, and this enables us to peer far more deeply into people's affairs than ever before. And this then poses the question of whether society will permit itself to use the technology available. This is a deep, all-pervading question which goes way beyond problems of management. However it does touch us to the extent of our having to comply with the law, whatever it happens to be at the time. And we find ourselves occupied with the following typical situations:

Should a bank divulge information to the income tax authorities on the purchase and sale of shares by its customers?

Should a hospital supply patient information to the driving licence authority?

Should a hotel supply guest information to the police?

Should a company inform a credit agency about its dealings with customers?

The list is a long one, but in every case it is a discussion of the law in a context of acceptable social norms, and not a discussion about the computer. All the computer enables us to do is to give thorough and perhaps prompt answers.

On the other hand, the danger of *involuntary* release of information is far less in the case of the computer. It is much easier to ransack someone's paper files than steal the corresponding tape and get it printed, or to access information by means of an on-line terminal.

All we can do with the problem of confidentiality is to be properly aware of the law and to take proper managerial steps to ensure that we comply with it.

As a footnote to this chapter, the text book on big-time computer gangsterism is Morris West's *Harlequin*. Fiction, but too close to possibility for comfort.

20 The corporate computing plan

Now we have come to the point where everything we have talked about must be drawn together into a single entity. And in doing this you are creating the single most powerful control device available to you. Every step that is taken in the computing effort must be specified in an overall plan. And if you don't have such a plan right now, the quickest way that you can get control of the situation is to start one.

Planning is a dreary business. How often are we interrupted in trying to salvage the day to tell the company planner what we'll be doing five years from now, how many people we'll be needing and how much budget! I don't even know whether I'll still be working here, or whether the company will even exist. I haven't even decided yet what I'm going to do this weekend. But not everyone can be allowed to stumble from day to day. Someone has to see the light at the end of the tunnel.

However, while it is difficult to plan the business operations far into the future, the new products, the territory, the premises, it is somewhat easier with computing, remembering, of course, that in the final analysis computing can only be a consequence of a more all-embracing company plan. And this in itself can have a catalytic effect in that, to do the job properly, a computing plan should force the company plan into existence; if not in a single document, at least as the answers to a lot of penetrating questions.

The plan should consist, not of a single volume, but of a hierarchy of documents, from a very thin, tersely-worded version in the desk drawer of the man at the top, down to wheelbarrows full of intricate detail parked in the programming areas. At every level the plan should be kept in loose-leafed files enabling you to change it easily, and acting as a constant reminder that it is meant to be changed. Never make the mistake of casting the plan in concrete. The essence of computing is discovering new details, any one of which could cause a change of heart. A plan, any plan, should be made to be changed. A lousy plan is much better than no plan at all, and its very existence enables a better one to grow out of it. And that's good. So there's no such thing as a lousy plan.

But what should it look like? Well, it would be nice if we could produce a standard framework and let you just fill in your own details. But failing that, what I am going to try to do in this chapter is go through the motions of a top-level version to give you something to improve upon. After that I shall make a few remarks about the versions at the lower and more detailed levels.

The top-level version

The top-level version of the plan should be created first, and written by you, perhaps with a little help. Since the version at every other level is a consequence of it this means that you are in charge of the situation. On the other hand if this version gets produced last it will of necessity be written for you by someone else down the line, and will consist of a simple-minded version of things that other people have decided. Just enough to get you off their back.

This version must by its very nature be thin. Fifty pages at the most, in contrast to hundreds or thousands at the other levels. It must be a readable, very concentrated version, containing a reference to every important aspect, but no supporting detail.

On the pages that follow are submitted a sketch of a top-level version. To give it a little shape and substance I have little option but choose a particular kind of organisation, and so I have chosen a manufacturing company. However it is not the detail of the sentences that is important, it is merely the example that they are intended to convey. It consists of four parts, and since much of the example becomes self-evident, most of the pages are omitted.

AMALGAMATED MATCHBOX MANUFACTURING COMPANY

CORPORATE COMPUTING PLAN

Contents

1. The corporate computing goals

The purpose of using computing in this corporation is to increase our annual profits and thereby pay a larger annual dividend to the shareholders. In order to achieve this we will:

a) Improve the service to our field salesmen and solve the problems of over-stocking, stock-outs, delayed dispatch and billing, by furnishing the office sales staff with terminals attached to an immediate and accurate survey of the contents of the warehouses, and the facility for entering orders as they are received.
b) Reduce labour costs and the costs caused by errors in carrying out engineering changes by harnessing the computer to our production planning department.
c) Reduce storage and transportation costs by creating a system for rationalising our entire distribution system.
d) Tie all new systems into our existing headquarters payroll and accounting systems as appropriate, eventually modernising the latter to take advantage of up-to-date equipment.

We shall implement the necessary systems in order of apparent profitability to the corporation, and shall take appropriate advantage of the state of the computing art to create common data files, thereby minimising the passage of data through the corporation and maximising its accuracy.

1

2 Operational level analysis

2.1 Corporate picture

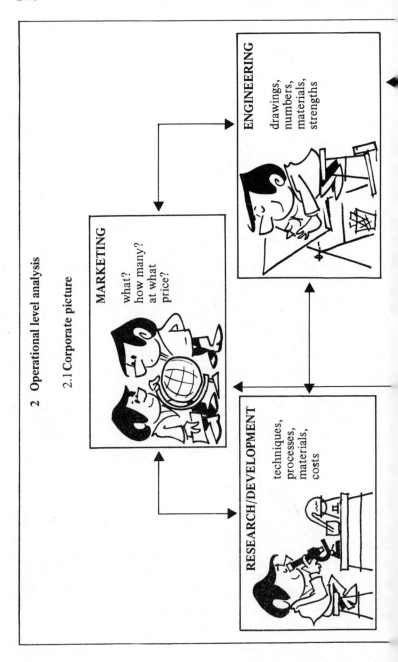

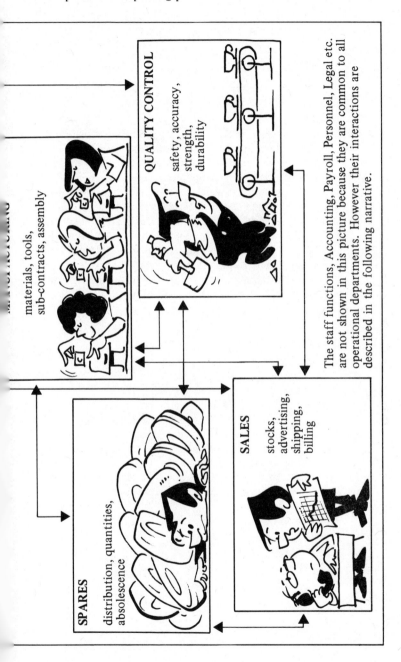

QUALITY CONTROL

safety, accuracy, strength, durability

materials, tools, sub-contracts, assembly

SPARES

distribution, quantities, absolescence

SALES

stocks, advertising, shipping, billing

The staff functions, Accounting, Payroll, Personnel, Legal etc. are not shown in this picture because they are common to all operational departments. However their interactions are described in the following narrative.

2.2 Marketing

Marketing is the forefront of the corporation. It is in marketing where the recommendations are made for the creation of goods and services that the rest of the company shall furnish. In order to undertake this task Marketing must be constantly aware of consumer requirements, competitive activity, technological innovation, product costs, government policy, legal factors, environmental factors and so on. To maintain this awareness requires, internally, a close working relationship with Research and Development and Engineering to know what is possible, and externally a lot of information about the market and its environment, and the means of dealing with this information.

Etc.

Marketing has developed the following procedures for dealing with other departments in the company:

2.2.1 *Research and development*

(a) R & D maintains an up-to-date manual of basic material and process prices for Marketing.

(b) R & D provides frequent reports of its research activity with particular stress on new invention opportunities as they arise.

(c) Marketing provides R & D with ideas to explore as it detects trends in the market place.

Etc.

4

2.2.2 *Engineering*

(a) Engineering provides a Preliminary Design service to Marketing including pricing and timing. The essential quality of this service is speed rather than detail.

(b) Engineering provides drawings, models, calculations and other services to Marketing in support of Marketing's presentations to company management.

(c) Marketing keeps Engineering appraised of its findings in dealing with customers and prospects as a means of early warning of new products.

Etc.

2.2.3 *Sales*

(a) Sales submits regular reports of business, problems, customer enquiries etc. as a means of feedback to Marketing regarding its past decisions.

(b) Marketing prepares material for market evaluations which are carried out by Sales.

(c) Sales passes on to Marketing information gleaned from the field concerning competitive products, and apparent opportunities requiring corporate action.

Etc.

2.2.4 *Accounting*

(a) Marketing provides Accounting with a monthly report of hours worked per project.

(b) Accounting is responsible for the preparation of pay slips for Marketing's personnel.

(c) Accounting provides Marketing with a monthly report of company expenditures per project.

Etc.

5

3 Managerial reporting superstructure

Action at the working level creates information which can be accumulated and used by management higher up the organisation, and requires information from management. Management reports are grouped into three classes.

3.1 Class A: Reports currently received from the manual systems at the working level

(a) *Assembly behind schedule* (Manufacturing)
A daily report due at 8 a.m. of the status in the assembly line compared with the production plan.
(b) *Customer out of action* (Spares)
A monthly report detailing the circumstances of each incidence of a customer who could not continue his operations due to the non-availability of a spare part.
(c) *Missed sales* (Sales)
A monthly report detailing the circumstances of each incidence of a missed sale, with recommendations for company effort to prevent a recurrence of a similar situation.

Etc.

3.2 Class B: Reports required in the future from the working level

(a) *Part fluctuation* (Manufacturing)

A monthly report of the level of stock of critical items over the previous twenty-four months, presented as a graph.

(b) *Overtime fatigue* (Manufacturing, QC and Personnel)

A monthly report showing the correlation between man-hours of overtime and incidence of bad workmanship.

(c) *Engineering change impact* (Engineering, Manufacturing)

A monthly report showing the correlation between incidence of engineering change and incidence of assembly behind schedule.

Etc.

3.3 Reports required in the future from other managerial levels

(a) *Materials unreliability* (R & D and QC)

A periodic report from QC to R & D containing incidence of materials failure, showing supplier information, composition, strength, impurities etc.

(b) *Personnel quality* (All departments)

A periodic report from all departments to Personnel containing analyses of employee performance against company training plans, academic qualifications etc.

(c) *Customer plant visits* (Sales and HQ)

A periodic report showing the effectiveness to the sales effort of visits by prospects to the R & D, Engineering and Manufacturing facilities.

Etc.

18

4 The firing order

The firing order constitutes the overview of the computer effort. It contains short descriptions of the systems to be implemented in order of implementation, and references to the detailed documentation of systems design, programming, training, running-in, operations etc.

The following are the system descriptions:

4.1 On-line Order Entry: OE 1

The most severe problem facing the company today is its sluggish response to customer requests and hence its steadily weakening competitive position; also the cost of accounts receivable. The purpose of the on-line order entry system is to create a numerical file in the central computer reflecting an accurate picture of the contents of the warehouses, and to attach this file to terminals in the sales office enabling the staff to respond to requests and confirm sales while the customer is on the phone. The system will initiate two profitable side-effects, reduced investment in stock and immediate billing, hence a reduced cost of accounts receivable.

The current cost to the company of poor sales response is incalculable but in the long run could mean the value of the company. The current investment in stock is $100 million and in accounts receivable $10 million. The goal is to reduce both by ten per cent within three years, after an investment of $2 million in system implementation. After OE 1 has been accepted and goes into production, the experience gained in creating and using it will be used as the point of departure for an improved version to be called OE 2.

Documentation to be produced:

OE 1 R System requirements document
OE 1 D System design document
OE 1 C Coding and checkout document
 T 17   Training document
OE 11   System installation and acceptance plan
OPS 23 Operational statistics report

20

4.2 Production Planning: PP1

The purpose of the production planning system is to reduce the staff of the production planning department, reduce the time taken to create plans, improve the quality of planning, reduce the errors due to engineering changes, and to provide an automatic basis for carrying out the plan and reporting against it.

The current cost of production planning is $2 million per annum, and the goal of the system is to reduce this to an annual cost of $½ million after an investment of $1 million in system implementation.

The system is to consist of a suite of basic routines containing general mathematical procedures and particular corporate information such as the current impact on facilities and learning curve data, and is to provide detailed planning paper for use in the factory, and marked cards for feed-back purposes.

4.3 Distribution: DIST 1

The distribution system project is an attempt to rationalise the storage and transport of company products and spares. The situation today is something that has been inherited from fifty years of de-centralised management and is responsible for significant losses to the company in terms of poor overview of stocked items, poor geographical spread of items, random choice of supply points and delivery routes, etc.

The current investment in warehouse buildings and truck fleet stands at $50 million and the annual cost of operations is $1 million. It is hoped to reduce the investment in warehousing by ten per cent and to hold the annual cost of operations to the current level. It is hoped that these aims can be achieved by an operational research study leading to the design of a company-wide distribution management system. A budget of $200,000 will be allocated to Phase 1, the initial OR study, and the details of Phase 2 will be decided after Phase 1 is finished.

21

The bottom-level version

Any word, number or sentence in the top-level version can expand into a paragraph at the next level, and end up as a volume at the bottom level. The bottom-level, or working-level version consists of all the coding sheets, flow-charts, progress reports, user documents and budget over-run explanations that are created by the implementation team. You can argue if you like whether this heterogeneous array of sheets of paper constitutes a part of the plan itself or the visible *results* of the plan. Either way, the essential point is that each one should be referred to at a higher level, and produceable at any discussion of the plan.

Intermediate levels

Depending on the size and complexity of your organisation, the ambitions of Computing within it, how far it has reached in its goals, how many problems it has encountered, there will almost certainly be versions of the plan lying between the top-level document and the working-level coding sheets. There is little point in speculating in this book on the nature of the intermediate versions. Although the bottom level will look uncannily alike from company to company, and hopefully so the top level, the versions in between could take on too many different guises to make speculation worthwhile.

Some may consist of sheets of paper in ring binders, again. Others may be charts stuck on the wall of the room in which you hold your periodic review. However, one factor will be common to all organisations, namely that the rate of change of detail will increase very rapidly from top to bottom. During the development stages the coding sheets at the bottom level change hourly with resounding audible expletives. But this is not reflected at all at the top, where changes of any significance will take place perhaps about once a quarter, and done so with decorum and all due ceremony.

Building up the plan

As I said at the start, you must create the plan from the top
down, each level calling for more detail at the next. However,
precisely because each level creates more detail and has the
opportunity of thinking of more aspects, items can pop up
that had been overlooked at the higher levels. Therefore the
evolution of a plan must be an iterative business. As detail is
produced at a particular level, the higher versions should be
checked to ensure that somehow or other they contain the
appropriate references. And when they don't, when a new
detail has to be inserted, the opportunity arises for a little
corporate learning. Why was the detail overlooked? What else
are we overlooking? What can we do to ensure that similar
details are remembered in the future? What impact has the
detail on costs and schedules?   Is there suddenly a need for a
major review? And what new fascinating fact does the man
at the top thereby learn about the computer?

Building up the plan is a never-ending process.

A corporate plan for computing is not something that we create once
to assuage some feeling of guilt.

Using it

A corporate plan for computing is not something that we create once to assuage some feeling of guilt, or as an outward and visible proof that management is really in charge, or to look good when the consultants come around. To have any effect, to justify the cost of producing it, it must be a living, breathing thing. It must be housed in loose-leaf binders, and any page must be a candidate for deletion or modification. In particular the top-level version must not become an object of sanctity. A top-level statement must not be preserved in the face of criticism in order to save its author's face. It must be stated right at the start that the whole computing exercise is a learning process for everyone concerned, manager and minion. There are no experts, and we are all in the mire together.

And probably even worse than defending a plan is forgetting it altogether. A plan can be produced in a fit of top-level enthusiasm, and foisted on a grudging or even rebellious work-force without adequate explanation or encouragement, and then promptly forgotten. Corporate dust will settle thickly on every version if the plan isn't made an integral part of its execution. And this gives rise to the famous managerial validity criterion known as the Dust Test; if you find yourself blowing dust off, something is seriously wrong. Go and find out what it is. It is probably disastrous. The corollary is known as the Paper Heap Half-Life, the time it takes before half the contents of an arbitrary in-tray can be thrown away without reading it. (You lose either way. If it's short you're on the wrong mailing lists. If it's long you'd better get in earlier in the morning.)

No discussion shall take place without producing the relevant documents, a sentence at the top-level, and wheel-barrow full of printout (God forbid!) at the working level. The top man must be coached by his subordinates not to indulge in discussions of the computer without getting out his ring binder. The top man must now allow any bright ideas to come into his room without the perpetrator pointing to chapter and verse in the plan. And if the idea is brand new, the most important question must be, what would be the impact on the current plan if we incorporated it?

A plan, to be of any earthly use, must be a living, breathing, daily phenomenon, whose existence makes a vital difference to the success of the enterprise.

Pruning it

At last, as this and that system finally gains acceptance and passes into the fabric of your organisation, you remove its details from the plan and add its name to the *In Memorium* column. It isn't really forgotten because the system keeper now has it in his tender care, but you won't need all the archaeological layers in your desk!

21 Getting organised

When computers were first thought of they certainly weren't intended to change the way people organised themselves. Why should the onset of automatic arithmetic threaten the nice, cosy way you have carved up the jobs and assigned the people? Goodness knows, it's difficult enough as it is to get a good organisation going, and it's impossible to find the right people. You have the historical problem, you've inherited a way of life from your grandfather's grandfather, and if you monkey with it you are going to upset all the over-thirties and the work will drop off. You've got the geographical problem, plants and warehouses around half the globe, each with its idiosyncratic boss. You have diversified into a clutch of heterogeneous divisions, and you're forced to have the headquarters in Philadelphia because your wife can't stand Chicago.

Then along comes the computer man who wants his say in the matter. The conflicts have already reduced your manoeuvring space to a nut shell, and the computer man probably has a friend who's an organisation expert. Just what you needed.

Why don't they leave you alone? You let them have all that equipment, which meant you had to delay one of your own pet projects for three years, the new headquarters building with the Rodin statue. You let them hire all these weird people. They got almost everything they wanted, even office space, but now they're banging on the door asking for status. You went along with producing the plan. You dutifully keep it in your top drawer. You have been digging into the details once in a while, asking an occasional smart question and getting the company lawyer all shaken up. Why don't they just get on with it? What is it about computing that's so special? They're a bunch of *prima donnas*. You wish you'd kept out of it.

Well one thing about computing is that it gets everywhere. Anyone can acquire it or get it thrust upon them. Computing is mostly an art and hardly at all a science. It's very much a creative phenomenon, though not entirely. There's no prescription for success, no mechanism for guaranteeing either that the bright ideas are all thought of, or that they are properly implemented. The history of computing is replete with fiascos — although, believe it or not, there are some brilliant successes which the press hasn't heard of.

Probably the only other item that gets everywhere in an organisation is the payroll system and the accounts systems that are attached to it. Although people in all departments are givers and receivers of accounting information, you have a special accounts department to take care of it. You don't let Research and Knot Inspection run their own Mickey Mouse accounting systems.

But the argument for computing is even stronger. Not only does the current version of the computing function affect people anywhere in the company, but ideas for future versions can also come from people anywhere in the company. No one has a monopoly of wisdom. And you don't have to know about the innards of a computer to understand what it can be made to do. A large number of the good ideas will come from the working level because it is here where the final outcome of all the planning, designing, implementing and training rests. These are the people who bear the brunt when a system goes into action. And these are the people who, in the long run, reap most of the benefit. But you can't get from brunt to benefit without doing something about it. You've got to arrange for constructive griping. When the system hits the fan for the first time the corporate air will be thick with feathers of confusion. Unless you are a one in a thousand exception your brand new system will contain all sorts of blunders, all the way from poor initial design to trivial last-minute coding errors, though nothing is trivial in computing. So to reach the goal that you all originally had in mind, the details of the blunders must be organised into an orderly flow back to the programmers. This is clue number one, remembering that the lifetime of the system will greatly exceed its gestation time, and that even after the original hullaballoo dies down, as the users get confidence that what they have works, there will be a constant, albeit thin, stream of new ideas for making it work better.

Clue number two is something we talked about earlier in a slightly different context; does your company provide an attractive career in computing? If computing consists of small groups of people scattered around the traditional depart-ments do any of these groups exceed the sort of critical mass that you need for a healthy professional atmosphere? Do the people feel isolated? Indeed alienated? Do any of the group leaders have a chance of the top slot in their later careers? Do the groups compete? Are they guilty of the age-old sin of duplication? Do they even have their own equip-ment? Incompatible equipment at that? From different manufacturers? Do you have a number of small machines instead of one large one? The list of questions is long, but most of the answers point in the same inevitable direction.

You may counter with at least two arguments, that tra-ditional department heads have delegated authority, and that the divisions are largely autonomous. Let's take the first one. It is true that department heads have to have the necessary authority to carry out the task for which they are responsible and accountable, but no department exists in isolation. Accounting receives information from everywhere in the company, and if they are to have a hope of survival there must be some uniformity in the way it's done. Engineering and Manufacturing can't be allowed to invent their own fancy method for keeping track of time under the label of departmental authority. Engineering doesn't invent a design release system and foist it off on Manufacturing, take it or leave it. There are plenty of examples of interdepartmental cooperation where the lines of authority become shadowy; there's no watertight rule for who decides. Many of the most important decisions in the working world are made without specifying how. This is a well-known fact of life that rarely seems to be admitted by the academic bystanders, and doesn't therefore get into print. And the reason is that the decisions are made by people, assisted or not by computers, not by formulae.

So, delegated authority we have, but within limits set by the other members of the corporate tribe, and this goes for computing as much as for the traditional functions. I doubt very much whether a department manager today would be allowed to get very far with this argument by the other department managers. You could probably stay out of this one and still win it.

But how about the divisions? Here the discussion isn't so obvious. There are too many variations on the theme. How functionally different are they? How far flung? How much autonomy do they really have? The US Air Force has bases around the world, but they all carry out a common task, and are heavily dependent on computing. It would be unthinkable to allow each base to do its own thing on the computer. Instead, the systems are created centrally and imposed on the bases. Is centralisation appropriate for your kind of business? If you are technically diversified into gear boxes, dairies and Christmas trees, what kinds of information do your divisions create or need in common? Even the payroll rules may be different, one from another. The only thing in common may be the computer itself. In this case you might find it appropriate to let the divisions go it alone, with a headquarters coordinator whose function it might be merely to keep you informed of how it was all coming along. You are still calling the shots, but divisionally and not corporately. Or the headquarters function might be a little stronger. It might operate the central equipment and be responsible for hiring and training the people; i.e. it could be the supplier of the basic product, allowing the divisions to use it at will, with some sort of internal contract and billing arrangement.

Whatever the relationship is at any time between headquarters and the divisions, you can bet one thing, the pendulum will swing. Put a gung-ho type in the headquarters slot and it will swing to the centre. Or the headquarters service gets so sluggish that you have a baronial revolution on your hands, and it will swing out again. If it doesn't swing, something's wrong. Computing is being ignored. Why? What's gone wrong? Time for you to assert yourself again.

Getting back to the main clues, when all the chips are down the inescapable decision is to put all of the computing functions into a single organisation, and to let that organisation report at a high level; the same level as the traditional departments. We wouldn't have said this in the early days, mainly because the subject never came up. No one posed the question, and the computer wasn't important then. It couldn't be; it didn't work well enough. As its reliability improved however, and its size, cost and span of applications increased, the level of attention rose, and by now it has reached the top.

But who's going to run it and how does he get his orders? Should you have someone who has arisen out of the foam of computing, or who has come up through the traditional organisation? Again, there is something to be said for both. But wherever he comes from, he is first and foremost a manager. There's no discussion about that.

The advantage of heading up computing with a company man is that you have a built-in assurance that the company will come first in the computing department. That attitude ought to permeate right down, especially if the department doesn't grow too fast. A company man would need some detailed training in computing matters. He would need to know fairly intimately what it's like to design systems and write programs, what a programmer's problems are, what he needs to do his job. He needs to know everything that you need to know, but in much greater detail.

The problem with bringing in an outsider, of course, is that it takes time to get to know the company. Where do his loyalties lie? What of his long-term career? With the company or with the computing profession? The advantage is that you are more likely to get a good technical staff. And you need this badly. If you present the same computing task to a thousand people you will get a thousand different solutions and they will vary enormously in quality and economics:

and few of them may be really first class. So a computer
man in charge means a greater probability of a good technical
solution, but unless you organise things properly you could
have the age-old dilemma of the right solution to the wrong
problem.

Even having a company man in charge is no guarantee of
attacking the right problem. Although he will lay his hand on
his heart and say that he has the best interests of the company there, his is only one man's view and we need a collec-
tive view. In either case you still need an innovation to tack
on to the organisation to make sure that Computing does the
right thing. Computing's task is to present options and then
to carry out the option, chosen by the company, to the best
of its ability.

The computer plan is essentially for the *implementation*
of a series of systems, and you are in charge of the plan. But
what the plan cannot provide for is the long-term system-
keeping task that follows. You won't be so interested in this
yourself. Once you have determined the strategy you ought
to be able to delegate the fine tuning to others. So to round
off the organisation you need a mechanism to collect all the
bright ideas for the evolution of the existing system, reject
the non-starters, select the promising ones, and arrange them
in an orderly sequence. Now whether this is done department
by department or corporately is up to you. A large company
will probably adopt the former, since it will probably have
systems keepers for each individual system, whereas a small
company may only be able to afford a single keeper responsible for all the systems. In either case it is someone's task to
do the collecting, sifting and prioritising; either a department
computing coordinator (perish the word!) or a corporate
computing czar. In either case these people *must* be company
people, and old ones at that. Every grey hair on their head
must have come from worrying detailed problems of the
company for a generation. Who might they be? Well, they
might be the next man in the top slot. They might be a
passed-over contender. They might even be an ex-incumbent
of the top slot who, for one reason or another, has decided
to step down. But whatever, they must be people highly

respected by their colleagues because their colleagues won't have the time to interfere daily in what they do. A healthy practice is to have quarterly meetings, chaired by you, of the department heads and the coordinator or the czar, to review progress, and to give you the opportunity of finding out whether the long-term aspirations of the plan are being fulfilled.

In short, you and the plan create the strategy for computing, up to the point of acceptance, while the system-keeping constitutes the tactics. And, hold on to your hat, as time goes on it is the system-keeping that dominates. The consequence of this is that, after some years of investment of time and energy on your part, you can start to delegate again until the millenium arrives when the whole thing is a

But you will only have something to delegate to if initially you invest time, energy and patience into building it up.

finely tuned instrument, and the birthpangs forgotten. Computing will then fall into place along with the rest, and become a traditional function and department, and your successor will have some other innovation to cope with and will be able to thank you profusely for not including computing in your legacy of confusion. Although you will only have something to delegate to if you invest time, energy and patience into building it up initially, and into creating a little enthusiasm for coping with the inevitable periods of despondency as things don't work out the way they were intended.

To complete the picture, what will the organisation look like if you use a service bureau? If the service bureau only provides the computer service you will still have a systems design and programming department as above. But if the service bureau does the whole thing, computing as an executive function won't appear on the organisation charts, nevertheless the rest will be the same. You still have the problem of deciding what to do. The company lawyer will now be included in the apparatus, and in essence, every message and instruction to the bureau must be couched within a very explicit legal framework. Perhaps this should be an extra reason for going outside for computing. The contractual relationship with the purveyor should give you even better control.

22 Taking the initiative

The purpose of this book has not been to philosophise about the wonders of computing, or to explain how computers work as an end in themselves, or to scare you with the problems of getting them to work, but to try to put you in the driving seat of computing in your own organisation. Everything we have talked about has this in view, but in case you've been drowned in information let us finish by compiling a list of techniques that you could or should employ in order to achieve this. There will be very little new in this chapter, so you can skip over it if you like and read the appendices. But if by now you haven't acquired your own pet list of things to do to become just as comfortable in the computer room as you are in the bottle-capping department then read on.

Time

How much time ought you to spend on matters computing? Are we talking about stealing five minutes a day from chit-chats with the factory manager? Or should you spend the first two hours of every morning reviewing the merry pranks perpetrated the night before in the machine room? Management is very much the management of time. There's never enough of it. But what have you been doing with it all these years? When Baron Courtebiche in *Clochmerle* reviewed the accounts of a lifetime he very much regretted how little he had spent on his secret charities. Being forced to re-evaluate your priorities in order to free up sufficient time to attend to computing may well force you to similar conclusions. That weekly run around the receiving bay, does it really do anything to help you run the company? Or has it been your Linus blanket ever since you got promoted out of the place twenty years ago? Should you instead have spent more time jollying up your more irate customers?

As with most other things the time you need will vary. If a new system is undergoing conception you ought to take the initiative to frequent reviews, though they may not be too long. If it is in the throes of acceptance you may have to fight your way out of other people's initiatives. On the other hand in mid-development or in periods of steady-state evolution the spontaneous demands on your time may be quite low, and you ought to be able to delegate affairs to the excellent arrangements that you have made for handling the details.

If you want a formula, the time you spend on computing should be proportional to the square of the danger to your company should anything go wrong. Concentrate on the danger points.

The corporate plan

If you don't yet have a properly organised plan for computing you can forget everything else. This is the key to the whole thing. Every discussion about computing that takes place in your presence must be in terms of the plan. You will have your thin version in your top drawer along with the latest version of the balance sheet, and at the jab of a pipe you can call for more detailed versions to be brought in in wheelbarrows – and out again. The plan, after you've got it all going, must be a natural by-product of the technical work, both preceding it and consequent to it. Unfortunately this is not always easy to arrange for. People hate to plan. Technical people hate to write, most of them. But what kind of basis for action is an unwritten system requirement or an unwritten computer evaluation?

Creating the plan and obtaining its enthusiastic backing from below may be a severe challenge to your managerial style, but you hold the trump card should it be necessary to play it. No plan, no budget.

Technical competence

You may well have created an elegant corporate computing plan, and indeed must do so, but when the last line and box are drawn, your first question must be, do we have people of the appropriate ability to carry it out? Or do we have access to them for the appropriate time periods? If the answer is not an unqualified 'yes' put the whole thing on ice until it is. You, yourself, will probably not want to be involved in searching for people, but you can easily require to be convinced that the chosen people are sufficiently technically qualified. Bear in mind always that the differences between computer people are enormous; much greater than you have been accustomed to in your other activities.

Budget sign-off

The hand that signs the budget rules the system. Every facet of the plan calls for the expenditure of funds, and every major step can be made the subject of a budget review providing you with an excellent opportunity of having it all explained. And it is important to point out that the explaining boot lies on the technical foot. It is their job to explain in your terms. If they use technical jargon switch off your hearing aid and keep your pen in your pocket.

However a budget review should not be totally one-sided. It also provides an opportunity for the technical people to view the organisation from your own lofty vantage point. Such opportunities are not unappreciated, and become part of your panoply of on-the-job managerial training techniques.

The more the technicians are able to evaluate their work from a corporate point of view, the better technical work they will produce. It will gain in maturity, expensive elegance will be more swiftly rejected and attention concentrated on squeezing the best technical solution from the funds available.

The monthly production report

When the systems are up and running their practical load on the computer becomes a part of the computer plan. The computer operations department requires a daily, weekly and monthly forecast of the time needed by each system for the ensuing year, say, plus a best guess as to the needs for the following year or two. This constitutes the basis on which Operations can make its plan for equipment capacity, operators, guaranteed levels of service etc. No forecast, no plan, bad service.

But once a forecast has been made, and accepted by Operations, it must be frequently compared with actual circumstances to determine how accurate it was, to measure Operations' performance and to bring out what problems Operations have encountered in carrying out its agreements.

If top management requires a monthly presentation of the preceding month's production statistics against the plan, it will ensure the existence of the plan. It will also ensure an alert operations manager who will do everything in his power to ensure top quality statistics. If you attend this meeting you will learn a lot, and if your attention is expected Operations will be on their toes in the machine room, even if you don't always turn up.

The client meeting

The monthly production report meeting is an example of a broader type of client meeting, a periodic meeting of the computing department and their clients where the corporate plan is reviewed against progress, in all major aspects of the plan — systems design and implementation, documentation, testing, training, acceptance and production running. Since it is a regular meeting, convened as a result of a plan, there is usually no difficulty in making it a reasonably calm, objective session as opposed to a vituperative exercise in mutual accusation. Again, your occasional presence will ensure that the meeting takes place and will enable you to keep on top of events.

Manufacturer visits

You should establish and maintain a relationship with the computer manufacturers at your level. An occasional visit to their design offices and factories will keep you up-to-date on current equipment, and this can be complemented by visits to their laboratories where you can obtain early warning of equipment to come. At the same time such visits will enable you to present the manufacturers with the long-term computing requirements of your company.

An associated idea is sometimes for you to attend a meeting of your users' group as an observer. These usually occur twice a year and provide a forum for exchanges of information between user and manufacturer. You would probably not want to play an active role, but the occasion will give you a large number of random insights into what is going on, what the problems are, how the economics are coming and so forth, and can help you establish useful contacts with respect to the next idea, that of associating with your birds of a feather.

Birds of a feather

The other companies in your industry and the other customers of your computer supplier constitute an invaluable masonry. You can maintain a correspondence with them, visit them once a year, embark on combined operations with them and generally take an active part in developing the right kinds of computing system at the right prices. Although you compete with the other companies at the level of design, quality, cost, reliability, sales response and so on, there is no reason why you cannot combine at the level of internal bureaucracy.

One side-effect of this is to find out how other top managements are coping with the problem of understanding and controlling computing in their companies.

The paper mountain

A very concrete, visible measure of the state of computing in your organisation is the amount of paper that comes out of the computer room door. Ask how much it is, and convert it to miles per year. Why is it so much, and what steps are being taken to reduce it? The answers to these questions should lead you to a lot of fascinating detail. The object of the exercise is not to save paper, but to reduce the computer cost in creating the data that is printed on the paper, and the human time spent in looking at it. Indeed if any time *is* spent looking at it. Here is one of the few opportunities management has of doing something that is directly measurable, so be a paper tiger and dig deep into the heap.

The NIH factor

One of the biggest human stumbling blocks is pride. This is an inherited survival factor that makes it possible for isolated groups to re-invent and re-develop, and thereby stay alive. But still today, if a thing is Not Invented Here it's no good.

Management's job is to distinguish between a genuine inability to use something already developed elsewhere and a refusal to do so because of one's pride in one's own work. Something invented in someone else's organisation could conceivably be better and cheaper than something your own

One of the biggest human stumbling blocks . . . .

people could do, as well as being already in existence.

But, beware. You don't want to crush the creative spirit of your people. Somehow you must strike a balance, but no one can tell you how to do it. This can only come from your personal managerial style.

Using your secretary

Make sure your secretary pays frequent visits to the ladies' room. That's where the real management decisions are made. In *Up the Organisation* Robert Townsend advises against having secretaries. This is wrong. It cuts you off from an invaluable and sensitive source of corporate information. (And, anyway, Townsend borrowed a colleague's secretary to type his book.) In *Corporation Man* Antony Jay talks about the king's dispersed tribe. The king's secretary operates a queen's dispersed tribe. It doesn't appear on the charts, but it is a powerful force in the organisation, and the good manager recognises the fact, and uses it.

The point of interest in our context is that the secretarial network can be used to detect discontent at the working level resulting from badly-installed computing systems. Before the discontent has had time to move up the formal organisation, you can find out about it from your secretary and can start asking anticipatory questions down the line.

The major questions

At every planned milestone, and at every new proposal, have a check-off list of questions. Here is a short list. If you don't like it produce a better one of your own.

Have we good enough technical people to do the job?
Have we provided them adequate tools: software, hardware?
Do they have to invent new technology?
Which activity is the least well-understood?
Who has done something similar?
Why can't we use their program?
How reliable are the time and cost estimates?
Why must it be on-line? or
Why isn't it on-line?
What standards are relevant?
What standards are missing?
What documentation is planned?
Have we a rugged back-up procedure?
Is the client satisfied that Computing understands the problem?
Have all the related departments been taken into consideration?
How is the previous system going?
Are we ready yet to take the next step?
Are all the legal problems settled?

Each of these questions emerges from the detail covered somewhere or other in the preceding chapters. There are plenty of others, and you will undoubtedly evolve questions of your own as you meet the detail.

Enthusiasm

There is an ingredient in all successful human endeavour which never seems to acquire proper recognition for the part it plays in that success. It is that catalyst of human energy known as enthusiasm. Enthusiasm isn't something that operates all the time, but it needs to be there at the right moments. You cannot legislate for it. But an activity entirely lacking in it is a still-born affair. Enthusiasm is a sort of social chemical. Like many human factors it cannot be measured. It probably can't even be directly observed, but we all recognise its presence. We see it in the faces of the people, the way they talk, the way they walk, the hours they put in on the job. And when the final chip is down, the last chart drawn and the last version of the budget compiled, if enthusiasm hasn't been kindled amongst the people working on the project you'll have a guarantee of failure; a guarantee of poor quality and late delivery until thy cup of anguish and thy budget runneth over.

Some people know how to inspire. Others don't. Those who do are born with it. Patton and Montgomery were magnificent examples, but you don't have to be in that class to get a successful computer project on the air. But if you don't know how to do it yourself, delegate it. But make sure it's done. So, last item on this list, create enthusiasm.

Conclusion

You will certainly be able to add your own pet techniques to this short list, but at least it gives you a point of departure. Whatever you do, don't assume that the computing people know what's best for your company. Probe, question, suggest, criticise – and above all withhold your signature. In this way you can eventually acquire the comfortable knowledge that computing is doing the right thing in the right way to increase the profits in your company, reduce its costs, or whatever criteria of success you see fit to assign. Every topic discussed in these chapters contains clues to the points of weakness. Search them out according to your own managerial style and minimise the incidence of negative surprise. And if you haven't got him already, convert or hire a capable, ambitious George Crudworthy and fight him tooth and nail.

. . . . hire a capable, ambitious George Crudworthy and fight him tooth and nail.

King MIDAS, or the low-down on information

In all the discussions you've ever had or are ever likely to have with computer people you will be confronted with a little set of terms that can cause a great deal of confusion. Nevertheless you'll rarely encounter an attempt at a definition, and even the computer people themselves often talk at cross-purposes about them, and way over the head of the person who is supposed to benefit from it all — the poor old manager. The terms in question are 'number', 'data', 'information', 'management information' and 'management information system'. The literature abounds with these terms. They are the basic objects of computing, as ore, coke and pig-iron are the basic objects of smelting. But managers of steel companies understand the latter far better than managers in general understand the former. But information is really far easier to understand than the reaction dynamics of a blast furnace. Therefore, since this is what computing is all about, you really ought to come to grips with it.

Information is a *commodity*, like money and materials. It has a *cost* and a *value*, and constitutes one of the fundamental aspects of the fabric of our society. But because it is less tangible than the other aspects, it is less properly understood.

Some basic definitions

At the root of the discussion lies the concept of number. Examples of numbers are 0, 1, 3,142, −273 and 1,000,000 but these are pure abstract entities and to be of any use have to be coupled with concrete ideas — which is why such pragmatic people as the Romans didn't have the number zero. You couldn't talk about nothing.

The next step is to arrange numbers according to some pattern, perhaps on a sheet of paper. Such arrangements of numbers tend to be called *data*. However there is no watertight definition, and we happily interchange the terms number and data without causing too much confusion.

But what do the numbers represent? When we start putting them in sentences we have something new. We have *information*. Examples:

Your credit balance stands at $2,785.65.

The warehouse contains 927 wheelbarrows.

Last week third shift worked 23 hours overtime.

NUMBERS + WORDS = INFORMATION

But how good are the numbers? Will you have a shock when you hear how little you have in the bank? How much overtime did third shift work the previous week? How much was budgeted? The next step is to add the expectations. Examples:

Sales for the quarter are five per cent over the corresponding quarter for last year, *but ten per cent below plan.*

Operating expenses for the month were $257,672 *against a planned $220,000.*

Warehouse levels of girders during the year dropped by twelve per cent *against a planned fourteen per cent.*

Now we are talking about *management information.*

INFORMATION + EXPECTATIONS = MANAGEMENT INFORMATION

Management information contains allusions to some plan created at the beginning of the year, say, and is the source material for managerial action. If the differences are within tolerance we make a mental note of the fact. If not, we leap for the phone.

The final step is a discussion of the managerial information system, but I shall defer this for a moment while I digress to dig a little deeper into the anatomy of information.

The formal orange and Thor's principle

An orange is identical to a glass of water. This is about eighty-five per cent true, and an analysis of the statement affords a fair analogy to information.

When the god Thor tried to drink the North Sea through a horn he discovered the principle that, to all intents and purposes, the amount of water in the world is infinite. An infinite stream flows past the living world, and most of it drains back into the (infinite) sea. But small amounts are arrested and incorporated into living organisms — amoebae, elephants and oranges. But water isn't a sort of biological afterthought, it is most of biology. An orange is about eighty-five per cent water, but it differs in one respect from the water in the glass. It is organised. The molecules of the water in the glass move around perfectly at random, and any drop in the glass looks like any other.

But the water in the orange is held in small cells. The cells themselves are arranged according to a very precise pattern, and within the cells the water molecules are arranged in a very precise pattern. In other words, an orange is a chunk of highly organised water.

The organisational substance of the orange is the element carbon, which is assisted in its task by very small quantities of other elements. And together they give to the orange its shape, colour, taste, strength, nutrient value and the ability to reproduce itself.

Formal and informal information

Like water, information exists in infinite quantities and flows continuously past us, mostly unnoticed. But finite bits of it can be trapped and organised for our use. It can be formalised. It can be given a structure and hence a value. And at that stage it is contained in informational oranges (files), constituting eighty-five per cent of the whole. The rest is structure, the file organisation that corresponds to carbon and nucleic acid.

What does informal information look like? There is, indeed, no limit to the form it can take. Snippets cut out of the newspaper. Scribbling on the back of an envelope. A telephone call. An idea that arose spontaneously in your mind while weeding the garden. Chit-chat at lunchtime. It all constitutes information. But it is not all equally accurate or useful to mankind. It all depends on the situation, the needs of the moment, man's innate genius, and so forth, what particular items of the infinite continuum of information are trapped and used. And it depends upon how frequently we want to trap it, whether we formalise it or not.

What does formal information look like? One could perhaps argue that the very fact of expressing a sentence, or even of conceiving a thought is a process of formalisation. But, while these are definitely first steps, a definition as early on in the process as this is not of much help. A usable definition of formal information must involve the conscious decision to trap the information on a regular basis, to perform the trapping and to act upon it in a procedural way, and must contain some notion of completeness.

For example we collect data about the hours people work. We do this regularly and completely. We probably punch it into cards, store it in files, print it on lists, compare it with standards. We process it and perform actions as a result of it. This is a typical example of formal information in the working world.

Not all formal information is put on the computer, however. The telephone book is a file of formal information. But as time goes on a growing amount of it finds its way on to the computer, and perhaps we could say that by the time it gets there it becomes super-formal.

We can observe, too, that over the long-term there is a natural human tendency to increase the amount of formal information. We are all familiar with the process. Someone has an idea. We ought to exercise a tight control over the lubrication procedures. He asks around and begins to sketch out some rough numbers showing the frequency of repairs due to faulty lubrication. He then computes the annual cost. A system is set up. Regular lubrication procedures are devised and the monthly maintenance report now contains a new column: the incidence of break-down due to improper lubrication. This is typical of the way we formalise things.

But we very rarely deformalise. It would take a brave soul to delete the lubrication column from the maintenance report, even if it became a column of zeros. It takes effort to do it, and there would be the argument that the situation would revert to that of the bad old days if we did.

So the formalisation of information is a one-way process, and this is one of the fundamental long-term causes for the increase in the computing bill. As a manager you should be constantly on the look out for possibilities of deformalising. Do we really need the monthly Late Take-off report? It sounded a good idea at the time, but do we really use it? Does it help us manage the company?

Storing information

We are all accustomed to storing information at the pre-computer stage. Informal information is stuffed into our hip-pocket while formal information is carefully placed in files, printed up in brochures, etc.

In the computer we have seen a rapid evolution of methods of storing information (all formal, of course). While it is far beyond the scope of this book to go into technical details, a superficial review is necessary to understand the core of the idea of management information systems.

At first all data was stored on punched cards, eighty characters to the card, and was kept in metal trays on rows of shelves. Not a method conducive to much processing, and we did the very minimum we could with it.

With the advent of magnetic tape we were able to do high-speed *serial* processing of data. We could sort data quite rapidly, and produce serial phenomena such as pay cheques and reports. A deep characteristic of the method of storage was that what went on the tape was pure *data*. The information *about* the data was implicit in the using programs, i.e. each record consisted of a series of numbers in an exact order, e.g. person number, rate of pay, number of hours worked, amount of tax, etc. This order was thought up by the person who wrote the program, and a consequence of this was that to each file of data there corresponded one program, and vice versa. There was little opportunity of combining data easily, and none at all of doing anything *random* with the data. No flexibility.

To solve this problem, magnetic discs and drums were invented, and the information about the data was removed from the programs and placed *amongst* the data, i.e. the data became *labelled*. This enabled a program to search easily and quickly *at random* for particular items without having to pass over hundreds of feet of irrelevant data.

This form of data storage earned the name *data base* and led to the creation of the enquiry program (e.g. seat reservations, inventory control) at the operating level, and to the possibility of similar programs at the managerial level.

Now we have arrived at the point where we can discuss the concept of management information systems.

Management information systems, MIS

As computing technology has developed and been harnessed to the operations of the working world, management has increasingly voiced the question: why can't I get my own hands on the computer? More and more of the formal information of the organisation is put into the computer, so it seems only reasonable that management ought to be able to use it in its own work in addition to its subordinates at the working level.

A full discussion of the reasonableness of this suggestion would take too long, however the upshot of the discussion is that at the working level one is involved with well formulated, repeated actions, while at the top level one plays a far more creative role in which it is really impossible to predict what one will do. Now in order to write a program at all one needs a precise description, and to make it economical it has to be frequently used. The working level satisfies both these requirements, but does the managerial level? How predictable is a general manager? How often does he repeat himself? If he wants to ask questions about his company's formal information via a computer program, someone has got to be bright enough to anticipate what questions he is going to ask. How much help can the manager be? Tough questions.

The basic question that management asks, in its creative moments, is 'What if?'

What would be the result of:

Giving more training to the salesmen?
Increasing the reorder levels in the warehouse?
Raising prices five per cent?
Lowering prices five per cent?
Opening up a new depot?

The burning question is, can we use the computer to help? Can we combine actual information about the company with a model of the business world that is sufficiently reliable to constitute a management tool? In short, can we build a viable MIS? Can we do it generally? Can we do it in specific cases? And if we can never do it completely, can we do it to a worthwhile degree?

This history of the development of these concepts has been fraught with muddled thinking, lack of definitions, poor understanding on the part of technicians of what management is all about, over-zealous selling, and a vast expenditure of money. The talk has been of managers with electronic crystal balls on their desks, peering into the economic future. But the people who have tried it have been badly let down. And at this point in time it is not clear what, if anything, will result from it all. A great deal of the technical substrate exists; the hardware, the data base management systems, the data definition languages and the data itself. But whether this will ever be profoundly usable above the middle management level is not at all obvious.

MIDS

Assuming that the idea of MIS is a viable one, is that what we really want? One of the ridiculous outcomes of the lack of communication between management theorists and managers is that the former are utterly convinced that the more information you give the latter the better decisions they can make. Instead of giving a thirsty man a glass of water, you turn the fire hose on him! People quickly get saturated. They can't cerebrate fast enough; the more you tell them the less they understand. What you would rather have is not an avalanche of information enabling *you* to make decisions, but a trickle of information telling you that decisions are being made by someone or something else in your name. What you need is not just a Management Information System, but a Management Information and *Decision* System: a MIDS.

Instead of giving a thirsty man a glass of water you turn the fire hose on him.

King MIDAS

But even that isn't enough. If you can automate a decision process, why not arrange for the appropriate *action* to take place? Why not create a Managerial Information, Decision and Action System: a MIDAS?

The mathematician-philosopher Alfred North Whitehead once said that we should use our heads as little as possible. And he was right. The remark may seem a little strange coming from a man who used his head far more than most people, but what he meant was that we should develop as many good habits as possible, relieving our creative energies for problems of importance. If we had to think about shaving, or tying our shoe-laces, we would be mentally exhausted before we reached the office.

In maximising our habits we are not restricted to the unaided human mechanism. We use all sorts of gadgetry in the process. Contrast the job of flying today's jet liner with the uninstrumented piloting of the Wright Brothers, or the running of an automated refinery with that of a manual refinery. And we don't necessarily need expensive equipment. Your wife doesn't rely on her memory when she goes shopping.

Generally speaking, once we have thought through a particular action and have decided that we will always follow the same pattern for a given problem, we can arrange for a combination of human and mechanical processes to take place automatically. However, it must be pointed out at the start that not at all decision processes are amenable to canned habit. We experience new situations with every passing day that require creative thought. If we didn't life would hardly be worth living.

There are many ways of making an automatic action system, but probably basic to all of them is a technique we call *decision tables*. A decision table consists of a set of questions, a set of answers and a set of consequential actions. The questions have to be phrased in such a manner as to admit only of yes/no answers. So you can't ask, 'What colour would you like?' or 'Have you stopped beating your wife?' Nevertheless, *binary* questions don't constitute any restriction on what you can ask, though they sometimes increase the amount of questioning. Indeed, the exercise involved in framing questions in this form helps to expose ambiguities and woolly thinking.

The questions, answers and actions may be arranged as follows:

Q1	Y	Y	Y	Y	N	N	N	N
Q2	Y	Y	N	N	Y	Y	N	N
Q3	Y	N	Y	N	Y	N	Y	N
A1	x							
A2		x			x			
A3			x			x		
A4				x			x	x

To each combination of answers there is one and only one action, and the actions are not arranged in any particular pattern. Note that the table contains all possible combinations of yes and no for three questions, ($2^3 = 8$), and that the number of actions can be different to the number of questions.

There are techniques for reducing the number of columns, often quite drastically, but explaining it won't add to the understanding. You don't need a computer if the number of questions isn't too great, but if you do use a computer you put the whole thing in a can. The popular press calls this 'letting the computer decide', but we know differently. It is we who have decided, the computer is merely delegated the task of searching the table and printing the corresponding action. No one can then monkey with it, and you can sit there with the comfortable feeling that people in the organisation are carrying out your instructions with much less scope for error than in the old days. Thus a MIDAS is a Management Comfort System. And you'd rather have comfort than information any day. You'd rather sit back and let King MIDAS loose to turn your sources of locked-up profit into gold.

The Holy Grail and its technological spin-offs

Let's get back for a moment to what we were saying about asking questions of a file of data in an MIS. However many *types* of data you collect they will be finite. The number of *combinations* of types of data will be finite, hence the number of possible questions you can be allowed to ask will be finite. However much data you collect and formalise, it will be finite. Therefore the number of possible answers will be finite. In other words, the computer man is telling the manager that there is an infinite number of questions that he *can't* ask, and answers he can't get.

So, if the manager is to be restricted to a finite set of questions that he's allowed to ask, what questions should they be? That in itself is a typical management question! He very rarely knows. Certainly at our lower levels of activity we have repeatable questions like, how's the cash-flow? How much overtime did we work last month? What was the Monday morning absentee report like? But at the level for which we're really paid, the creative level where we move the company forward with vigour, how can we know what we're going to ask? Particularly since it might take six months to write the program. What questions are you going to ask in six months time, or what hope is there that Computing can come up with some sort of general question-answering system?

Now I have implied the need to answer a 'general question'. By this I mean a question about any of the (finite) allowable attributes, couched in a sentence which is as free of restrictions as possible. I stipulate this because we do not want to restrict management in its freedom to communicate or express itself.

A manager would really like to ask questions of the computer the way he does of other people. However, spoken sentences are usually so ambiguous that it would not be possible to write a program to 'understand' them. Communication between man and machine can never be better than in a very restricted version of man's native tongue. However,

even here the restrictions might be such that after a short
training period the manager is comfortable within them. He
might be allowed to say:
'Tell me the names of the books by Melville', or
'Give me the titles of the books that Melville wrote',
whereas he may not be able to say:
'Melville wrote some books, I think that's his name, but
I'll be goddammed if I remember them. Do you?'

Sentence parsing by computer is exceedingly difficult.
Millions of dollars have been spent on the automatic trans-
lation of natural languages, with no discernible result. It really
seems senseless to allocate scarce resources to solving the
kinds of problem posed by the third example. This seems to
fall into the same category as the automatic reading of hand-
writing.

Closely connected with the problem of sentence parsing is
that of file structuring. Each proper noun in a sentence is an
attribute in a file, whereas the other parts of speech become
instructions to the program about what to do with those
attributes. Consequently the two fields of research have
really become one. Progress is being made, but whatever level
of success is reached, further work will always be required.

But whatever success we have on the computing side,
King MIDAS is ultimately a *management* problem. The
manager must be subjected to the same scientific scrutiny as
any other computer application. He is just as much an anthro-
pological curiosity as the head hunters of Borneo, and with
all the file-structuring success in the world, without a managerial Margaret Meade it will be of little avail. There are two
formidable obstacles to any overt corporate anthropology,
firstly, the lack of awareness amongst managers of the need;
and secondly, the problem of studying a manager without
changing his manner of managing. As we said in Chapter 9,
if he knows he's being watched he will act a role. There may
be subtle ways of overcoming these obstacles. As the computer tools become available, an individual manager will work
with programmers in an experimental environment, gradually
homing in on a program that suits him. But how useful will
the program be to his colleagues? Or his counterparts else-

where? Today we really do not know.

An interesting parallel to this problem is that of on-line process control. For as long as we have been processing materials, since the first bronze flowed from the first primitive furnace, man has always understood enough about reaction dynamics to control the process himself. Consequently, when the idea of using the computer to do the controlling first came about in the 1950s, process-control was regarded as a computer problem. But after a few failures it became quite clear that we did not indeed understand enough about the process after all, and the subject became a reaction dynamics problem instead. Similarly, computer assistance to high-level management is now passing from being a computer problem to a management dynamics problem.

However, there have been some results. There are in existence today some simple, somewhat general-purpose, management information systems, some written by the manufacturers and some by the users. They all suffer from the problems discussed here, however, but as these problems are gradually partially solved, the restrictions will become less irksome and the generality will increase, as will the amount of information at our disposal. There will always be an infinite number of questions which we cannot ask, but this will become less and less a serious criticism as the list of questions we can ask becomes longer. After all, there has always been an infinite number of questions which the human mind has been unable to answer, but with increasing knowledge of a finite realm, our quality of life has continued to improve, though it will never reach any 'ultimate' level. Similarly, as the generality of question answering increases, and management information becomes progressively more available at the creative level, our standard of management will continue to improve, although it, too, will never reach any ultimate level. As Pope said two hundred years ago, 'The proper study of mankind is man'. This is truer than ever today because we have computers!

Whether King MIDAS will ever become a reality, or whether he will always remain the philosopher's stone of a sort of twentieth century managerial alchemy, or a Holy

Grail, still remains to be seen. Whichever you anticipate personally, however, it is my opinion that he is a goal well worth pursuing. You may not catch him, but in trying you will acquire a lot of unexpected and valuable knowledge.

Captain Cook went out to observe a transit of Venus and came back with the Pacific Ocean. Neil Armstrong went to the moon and came back with the teflon frying pan.

The computer as a survival factor

'This strange disease of modern life'
Matthew Arnold

When the Roman army overpowered Veii, their first Etruscan victim, only ten miles or so from the Capitoline, they were utterly unaware of the fact that they had taken the first step of seven hundred years of empire building, and when the Wright Brothers were building the first aeroplane it is doubtful whether they had Boeing or Pan American uppermost in their minds. Likewise, IBM and NASA were probably far from Charles Babbage's thoughts as he wrestled with his first difference engine.

Computing has been no exception to the rule of historical happenstance, the benevolent (and sometimes not so benevolent) outcome of chance interactions between people, ideas, equipment and problems. No one has really been in charge. There have been digital dinosaurs galore. To a great extent serendipidy has been our guide and few of the grandiose predictions of the fifties are to be found amongst the realities of the seventies. At a conscious level this serendipidy is based on a deep yearning in the human breast to do automatic arithmetic. At a much deeper level it is based on the need to survive as the species civilised man. This final chapter, which has nothing whatever to do with management, is an attempt to explain this; to portray the computer in philosophical terms.

To begin with, society is owed an explanation of the explosive growth of computing capacity, a growth rate far exceeding that of the motor car, aeroplane or television set. There were no computers in 1948, two in 1949, 10,000 by 1960, several hundred thousand by 1970, and an uncountable number today. If you multiply these raw numbers by memory size and arithmetic speed the growth is even a couple of orders of magnitude greater. Technology made the growth possible, but what caused it? The answer is that for about 150 years there had been a latent need for computers that technology was unable to satisfy, and that had built up to bursting point by the time electronics reached the necessary level of reliability. Really we need the first computers when people were gathered together in the first factories and began to ride in the first trains. We needed the first computers when the numbers implicit in the commercial world started to get big. Babbage was not ahead of his time, it was technology that was woefully behind. The application of brass and steam was not universal.

We invented the computer because we had to. History was on the move, although no one was particularly aware of it at the time, hand-in-hand with biology. The whole thing was inevitable. The modern world was mutating, but no one realised it any more than a new generation of evolving giraffe notices his elongating neck.

What was the nature of this mutation? What caused it? Was it a beneficial one? What would have happened if it hadn't taken place? If it was meant to do anything was it in time? The idea poses a lot of very pertinent questions, and their answers serve as a useful backdrop against which to introduce some practical ideas.

Mutations are the elements of evolution, and evolution is the process of adapting to change in order to survive. Although we usually think of it in terms of animals and plants, evolution is a phenomenon common to just about everything that *homo sapiens* puts his hands to. Shoes and ships and sealing wax have all evolved in response to changing environments, and so have our ways of handling information – the stuff that computers are all about. The essential problem with this particular evolutionary event, however, is the speed with which it has had to take place.

But what's the problem? The problem is that in the normal evolutionary situation the species adapts to suit a changing environment, while in our case we are trying to fix up the environment so that the species can remain oblivious of the fact that it is changing. What we don't know in the long run is whether it will work.

At the centre of the problem we have *homo sapiens* in modern dress who feels he's moved a long way from his savage ancestors, but who really hasn't moved a cosmic inch. Indeed he still finds savage contemporaries in yet undefoliated necks of tropical woods whose children can be brought to the so-called civilized world, clothed and educated, and in one generation jump the thousands of years of technological development that separate the two. So modern man is only modern in the trappings of life, the physical and intellectual trappings. He is not modern in any biological sense, compared with contemporary primitive peoples.

What is of particular interest to us in this discussion is that the innate ability of both primitive and modern man to absorb and process information is the same. To be sure, education forces modern man to sharpen his mental information-processing faculties somewhat; he can remember all the products up to 12 times 12; he can read a map; he can cope with the lights and dials in a jet aircraft cockpit, but none of these examples is very far removed from primitive man's ability to remember his way through a jungle. Certainly neither is capable of remembering the details of a thousand-man payroll!

The problem, in short, is that man's mental faculties have not kept pace with the changes in his environment. Even if brain of the human variety were conceivably capable of vast, reliable memory, given the necessary embellishments, time has not allowed the necessary evolution to take place.

The cerebral state of man today is a product of millions of years of evolution in what we are pleased to call a primitive environment; an environment characterised, for our purposes, by very little usable information. In this environment he has lived in small groups, moved short distances at low speeds, had a very simple economy, practised hunting or simple agriculture, fought very limited wars and so on, while the amount of information that he has needed to process in order to accomplish his goals has been of such a nature that his brain could cope with it. But in recent times, geologically this morning in fact, man has created a completely different environment, one of large cities, busy streets, technological medicine, solar distances, space-gravitational speeds, global wars and international ignorance, misunderstanding and distrust of colossal proportions.

The usable information generated by man's modern environment is much too vast to be handled by the unaided brain. In other words man is not fitted for survival in the environment of his own creation and he would rapidly become extinct, crushed beneath the weight of necessary but unmanageable information. So in order to survive, he has had to take a series of steps towards coping with or shielding himself from this information. At first, marks on clay tablets, then writing on papyrus and paper, then printing, number systems and mathematical techniques, simple calculating machines, punched card equipment and finally computers; an evolution of mechanisms whose job it was to absorb the information generated by the created environment and reduce it to quantities typical of the primitive

A sort of shell or buffer, with man on the inside . . . . .

environment. We can picture it as constituting a sort of shell, or buffer, with man on the inside, relaxing in primitive splendour sipping the information concentrate that drips down on him, while his real environment on the outside bombards the buffer with a dense shower of raw information.

In short, we are creating a buffer with which to shelter ourselves from our true environment and simulate our primitive environment so that we can go on happily surviving without having to do much evolution. We may compare this idea with today's airlines. Outside it is 60 below in a 600 knot gale, while inside all is ease, comfort and martinis. It is the creation of the building blocks of this information buffer that has constituted the subject matter of this book. So by way of a link to the practical details allow me to enlarge on this idea for a moment and really try to bring home the importance of the adjective 'primitive', because, as I see it, here we have one of the fundamental criteria for success in the design of any practical information system.

Consider the simplicity of picking a flower from your garden. You stoop, pluck a rose and place it in your lapel. This is a primitive act. Neolithic woman probably did much the same on her way back from the first cornfield. It is a natural, spontaneous, human thing to do. It involves no one else. It is confined to you and your immediate environment, a garden, some flowers, trees and the sky. You adorn yourself with nature and that is that.

Now take a trip to the city. You stoop and pick a buttonhole from the flower lady, a coin changes hands, and again you have adorned yourself with nature in a way which, to you, is just as primitive as in the garden. But there is a slight difference; the flower did not grow in the street. To get it there some fairly simple organisation was at work involving certain human relationships and habits, transportation, economics, horticulture, climate, bound together by a modicum of information. The flower lady habitually fills her basket at a particular stall in the market, probably from the same wholesaler every day. She knows from experience the type and number of flowers to buy, at what price to buy and at what price to sell them. The total requirements of all the flower ladies is known to the wholesalers who transport the flowers *en masse* from the nurseries, and the wholesalers' needs are similarly known to the growers. This chain of goods and information is an example of what we call a system. In this particular case it is a system whose volume is a function of perhaps three main sets of variables, namely the predictable seasonal cycles of production, the much less predictable vagaries of the weather and the slowly changing population of city dwellers.

When you stoop to select your buttonhole, however, the existence of the system is in no way forced upon your attention. You are aware of the existence of the seasons, this is a part of your primitive life, so you know what flowers to expect at different times of the year, but you are not made aware of the chain of events, the sets of relationships, the economics or the information involved in bringing you your buttonhole. You have been involved in as little effort as in your garden.

You then enter the premises of a travel agent and ask for an airline ticket to New York where you have been invited to lecture this coming week. You tell the agent the day and the approximate hour at which you would like to arrive. Using a little keyboard machine she selects the appropriate flight and enters your name on the list of passengers. She then issues you a ticket, and some money changes hands. The entire transaction takes only a few minutes, a little longer than buying a flower, but not excessively long. The business of buying a ticket to New York appears to be as simple as picking a flower in your garden.

This is because we have made it appear that way, but the reality behind the façade is extremely complicated. Again we are faced with a system, but there is one essential difference between this system and the one for getting flowers to the city and out on its streets. The difference is the amount of information involved. In the flower system much of the information resides in the heads of the people involved, while some of it is written down on pieces of paper.

In the seat reservation system this is not the case. Aircraft land and take off in New York every minute of the day, containing hundreds of passengers. New York is a very dense point on the global airways network. Some of the passengers booked months in advance, others were wait-listed at the last minute against the possibility of an empty seat. Food has to be prepared and delivered on time. Some of the passengers require wheel chairs, others have babies and need cribs, others again are on special diets. Some passengers had purchased their tickets from one airline but are flying with another, and a special book-keeping transaction has to take place. There seems to be no end to the types of information that this system has to cope with, nor to the magnitude of that information. Yet each individual is presented with an image of the airline in which he is made to feel their sole concern. All is ease and comfort. All is primitive.

The seat reservation system is an integral part of our information-absorbing buffer and is perhaps today the best example of what has been done so far to protect the human organism from the chaos of information that the modern world needs in order to function.

It is, of course, anything but primitive. Nowhere in the system is the human brain used to retain or transmit information, and paper is used only as a by-product. The information on your ticket is only a copy of that held in some central electronic device. If you lose your ticket the system does not lose any information, and you can very easily obtain another.

Instead of brain and paper the information buffer uses electronic storage devices coupled to computers which move the information about as needed.

An essential point to be made is that in many cases we do not replace the brain and paper by automatic devices because they are cheaper, faster or more reliable (which they are) but because we have no option. It is not a question of degree but of kind. We do not carry out a comparison between human and machine, and choose one over the other; the possibility of using the former is now out of the question.

At this point some people begin to get a little emotional. They think we are saying that people are no good. And really this is true. We are not good in situations involving more information than our ears and eyes can receive, or our brain can process. This is no reflection on humans as humans. In fact it is a compliment. It says that although humans have been trying to perform the work of machines for millennia they have not been too successful. That is to say, humans are different from machines. Now that we have permanent-memory machines humans are too different to compete at all. Instead of opposing machines as some sort of supplanter of humans, we should welcome them as liberators of man's short amount of allotted time, enabling us to use our freedom for more human endeavour.

I chose the airline reservations system as an example of the information buffer because of its ease of description and because of its relatively successful implementation in the short history of computing. Although it is still quite easy to find a crack in the edifice. If, instead of booking to New York, you wish to tour the country giving a lecture in each of twenty cities on alternate days, the system will not devour the request quite so quickly. You will almost certainly be asked to come back later for your ticket. No flower; not primitive. It is however, only a question of time before a computer will be programmed to arrange itineraries on the spot, and to print tickets immediately.

There are many other systems operating today which together comprise the information buffer. Some of these have a direct impact on the private citizen while others operate behind the scenes in businesses, in factories and in government services. We cannot build modern aircraft or send rockets to the moon without computers. Our income tax returns are scrutinised by computers. Many of our bills are paid accompanied by a punched card. Our subscription magazines are addressed by computer. School reports are generated in part by computer. No insurance company or bank of any size can survive without placing much of its operations on a computer.

These, then, are the building blocks of the information buffer. And we continue to build this buffer in order to remain afloat in the sea of information created by modern life.

I would like to quote a short passage from Arnold Toynbee on this subject. He says:

'Man's new man-made artificial environment is something that has been making me think furiously. We started creating this artificial environment in the act of becoming human — i.e. when we made the first artificial tool by chipping a nature-given flint, but, by now, our man-made environment has effaced and replaced our natural one. We have now put ourselves in a position in which we are up against (i) practically infinite quantity in everything that we have to deal with, and (ii) practically infinite material power in all our actions.

In my piece about Namier*, I did suggest that the computer might be one of the tools for doing the job of coping with the *djinn* that we ourselves have conjured up. I am encouraged to hope that the computer may be a tool that will be equal to helping us in our present fix. But, as I see it, the job itself is a spiritual one, because all tools are morally neutral: they can be used at will for either good or evil, and the effects of potent tools are proportionately serious, one way or the other. Human beings now have almost unlimited power; if we are to avoid using this for self-destruction, the average human being has to raise his or her sights to the saints' elevation. Can we do it? And, if we can, will we do it? In science and technology there seems to be no limit to what we can do, and have the will to do, but in morals we are still in the Palaeolithic Age, not in the Atomic Age.'

Now I am not competent to discuss the question of the historical development of social morals, however I think that what one has to look for is a sharp acceleration in moral evolution to accompany the sharp acceleration in the rate of technological achievement that we have seen in recent years. Until this century, progress was made rather slowly. Discoveries of science were few and far between. Aristotle was born in 384 BC but it was not before the fifteenth century AD that the idea of careful measurement was proposed by Nicholas of Cusa. Again, even If Leonardo was the first to dissect corpses, it took two more centuries before Harvey was to discover the circulation of the blood. There were, of course, reasons for this. Harvey gives the clue when he says 'the Authority of Aristotle has always had such weight with me that I never think of differing from him inconsiderately'. Whether it was Aristotle himself or the fear of the Church, the fact remains that scientific progress was painfully slow.

*See *Acquaintances* by Arnold Toynbee

Moral progress was also slow. It was six hundred years after Christ before any other major religious figure was to appear, since when there has been no other.

So we can claim that moral and scientific progress remained more or less hand in hand. Thousands of millions of people came and went but very few of them did anything.

But what has happened in the twentieth century? Indeed since 1940? In technological matters what used to take a century now takes a decade. We have suddenly shrunk the technological time scale by at least an order of magnitude. If you plot 'progress' against time you find a very sharp upturn about the year 1940. To represent progress you can take the power of things, their size and speed, the number of people participating, the financial investment, the rate of passing of legislation. All the objectively measurable parameters are rising very steeply in the twentieth century where they have been more or less constant over most of recorded history.

Some dramatic examples, of course, are the power of explosions, the size and speed of aircraft, the numbers of motorcars, the ease and cheapness of telephoning around the world, the discoveries of pure science and the development of computers.

But is there any evidence that moral progress has undergone such an acceleration in the last quarter century? When a man is bound, hand and foot, it is of no importance to society what his moral calibre may be. When he is armed with a bow and arrow, society needs a modicum of moral restraint on his part. When he is armed with the atom, society needs a megaton of restraint. If we need new moral tools to cope with the moral problems posed by the new technology there simply has to be an accompanying moral acceleration. The question is then, what significant signs are there to show that the rate of moral development has taken a sharp upwards turn since 1940?

There do not seem to be any such signs. However, they may be there, but we are blind to the history being made around us. So let us suppose that we are not going to blow ourselves to bits and that the tools for coping with the problems of the created environment are worthy of discussion.

Toynbee talks of practical infinities of material quantity and power as the fundamental problems. I would like to add a third, the practical infinity of information. There is an infinite amount of information in a box of matches, even though it is information of little value. Clearly there is an actual infinity of useless information but as the sizes, speeds and complexities of the facets of the created environment increase, the amount of useful information required for their control increases, and it increases much more rapidly than the facets themselves.

Consider, for example, the question of mutual relationships between individual people. One man sitting alone in the desert has no relationship with anyone else. Two people have one relationship. Three people have three relationships. Ten people have fifty-five relationships, while 100 people have 5000. While the number of people increases in a straight line the number of relationships increases as the square, that is to say, ever more steeply. It is in this way that the amount of information increases as the number of facets generating it increase. To survive we must control, and to control we must absorb information. Even if no one blows us up internationally, we may yet be blown up by the pressure of inanimate events.

These are not philosophical problems but very real ones that face the politicians, managers, scientists and other manipulators of our daily lives. Because if the people at that level do not attempt to temper technology with morality whom do they expect will do it? In particular the people who will be deciding what computers shall be used for are also going to have to decide whether what they do is ethical. They will have a great deal of information about people, and information, as we well know, can be put to evil uses.

In this concluding chapter I have attempted to provide a historical-cum-biological reason for the invention of the computer and discussed the background to the ethical problem it creates. In doing this I offer two fundamental criteria for the proper use of computers, to which all technical criteria are either subordinate or consequent; namely, a computer application must appear primitive to the individual user and must behave ethically towards society. And the former ensures the latter, at least from the technical point of view. Primitivity implies human control and hence provides no excuse for unethical consequences.

In the final analysis, when all considerations of profitability have been taken care of, the criterion of primitivity is top management's essential task. If you delegate it, what hope have you of success in using the computer?

Index